# EYE TO EYE
# HEART TO HEART

# EYE TO EYE
# HEART TO HEART

## Elaine L. Jack

Deseret Book Company

Salt Lake City, Utah

**Library of Congress Cataloging-in-Publication Data**

Jack, Elaine L., 1928–
    Eye to eye, heart to heart / Elaine L. Jack.
      p.  cm.
    Includes index.
    ISBN 0-87579-603-6
    1. Relief Society (Church of Jesus Christ of Latter-day Saints)
I. Title.
BX8643.W4J33    1992
267'.449332 — dc20
                         91-47573
                             CIP

Printed in the United States of America

10   9   8   7   6   5   4   3   2   1

To my husband, Joe,

my support and companion in our life adventure,

and to our sons, Dave, Bill, Eric, and Gordon,

whose strength and stories I draw on.

# Contents

## Tools for Touching Lives

## Personal Vision

# Acknowledgments

The welcoming invitation of women who had confidence in asking me to share my experiences and viewpoints with them has made this book possible. Elder Marvin J. Ashton, chairman of the board of Deseret Book, kindly inquired, "When are we going to have a book from you?" Editors and staff of Deseret Book, Eleanor Knowles and Sheri Dew, Kent Ware and Emily Watts, opened the door further with their design and editing skills.

Relief Society study guides, especially those cultural refinement lessons on personal virtues, reinforced ideas taught in my home—look for the best in the world around you, seek the finer things of life. Shirley W. Thomas, formerly a counselor in the Relief Society general presidency, nurtured and encouraged my thinking, without regard to cost in time or effort to herself. My son Bill has been a sounding board for my ideas through the years.

Carol L. Clark, presently Relief Society administrative assistant and long-time friend, with a genius for probing meanings of words and applying scriptures to present-day needs, has helped me clarify my expression and bring new insights to classic topics. Helen Pehrson has provided untiring service in typing manuscripts and keeping the president's office running smoothly. Mary Gifford in the Church Historical Department continues cheerfully and efficiently to research sources and provide background information. Board member Cherry Silver has competently selected, arranged, and given first editing to these chapters.

# *Preface*

What we as human beings do within our spheres of influence are generally small things. We do not effect major change with one act or word. It may seem a small thing to talk heart to heart and see eye to eye, but the sum of such small things creates powerful results. Our gestures of kindness to each other, our pledge to live good lives, our efforts to make our homes solid and nurturing — all these contribute to the unfolding of God's eternal plan.

The Lord has granted me a feeling deep in my heart of warmth and concern for women. I have prayed for the capacity to form relationships with women wherever I meet them. I try to see things as they are experiencing them, to feel what they are feeling.

I envision the women of the world not in abstract, distant generalities. Rather, I have a mental reservoir stocked with happy memories of little moments with fascinating individuals.

In them and the stories they tell of their sisters, I have found many small treasures. I have learned from these women that to understand heart to heart and see eye to eye is a magnificent blessing and a gentle gift from God.

# Qualities of Life

# *Brightness of Hope*

I once asked a number of friends to share with me their favorite words. What began as a point of conversation soon became a period of testimony, for my friends suggested such things as *commitment, family,* and *love.*

I've reflected since that time about what my own favorite word might be. *Rejoice* is a major contender, but I think *hope* wins. To me hope embodies happy feelings, anticipation of good things, the best of the gospel, and zest for life. The word is embedded in the instructions of Nephi to followers of Christ: "Wherefore, ye must press forward with a steadfastness in Christ, having a perfect brightness of hope, and a love of God and of all men." (2 Nephi 31:20.)

"A perfect brightness of hope": what a light, ebullient phrase that is! I've stood on a mountaintop at sunrise and thought of that phrase. It moves and warms me. Hope—think what it does to the soul when we feel it. Hope—think what it does for the world when we act on it.

Since my call as Relief Society general president, I've met hundreds of Latter-day Saint women, received sheaves of their letters, and attended meetings in many places with and about women. I've learned a lot. One of the most important insights I have gained is that many of our sisters have lost hope. I see and hear evidences of this far too often—and it grieves me.

Some women have said:

"How many dates do I have to go on to find an eternal partner?"

"I am no longer needed. My family is gone. What good am I?"

"I don't get any support from my husband. I have to take care of everything related to church and children myself."

Such despairing comments make me sad because a life without hope is not life—not in the gospel sense. After Moroni had witnessed the destruction of his own family and all his friends and people, he wrote to the Lamanites: "And except ye have charity ye can in nowise be saved in the kingdom of God; neither can ye be saved in the kingdom of God if ye have not faith; neither can ye if ye have no hope. And if ye have no hope ye must needs be in despair." (Moroni 10:21–22.)

For me, to live in despair is not to live. I cannot imagine life without hope. Perhaps this is because I learned early that the personal quality of hope is essential for righteous living. In fact, hope is one of the personality traits of godlike men and women. Paul explained that members of the Church who wish to live "acceptable unto God" are in part characterized as those "not slothful in business; fervent in spirit; serving the Lord; rejoicing in hope; patient in tribulation; continuing instant in prayer." (Romans 12:1, 11–12.)

To me it is very important that "rejoicing in hope" is on the list of godlike characteristics, especially because we benefit so much from the comfort and happy expectation of hope in these tumultuous times.

Recently I read an article about a Cambodian family who endured unimaginable suffering. At the end of a particularly arduous day, the mother gathered the family together and taught, "Remember, children, hate does not end with more hate but with love. And from that we take hope. Without love and hope, our lives will be empty." What a wise mother!

My own dear mother taught me a lot about love and hope. She was ill for many years, yet she was always a bright, hopeful person. She taught me to recognize those who are "acceptable unto God" by the evidences of their belief in their attitudes and actions. Mother knew that it is hope that helps us rebound.

My niece Karen's children are close in age. Since Brad, now six, nearly drowned two years ago, he has required much extra care. Her father-in-law died about the time her mother entered a nursing home. Shortly after her mother died, her father remarried. And during all of this her husband has been starting up his own business.

As Karen knows, as we all know, daily living can be draining. The demands on women seem to multiply. Personal lives can be in terrible chaos. Yet hope stands as a beacon, warm, steady, and inviting. It is reassuring to me that this quality I enjoy so much is also requisite for those who would follow the light and life of the Savior of the world.

## Hope Matters

I testify to you that your hope matters. May I suggest three reasons why:

*First: Hope, charity, and faith are very closely related.* Paul concluded his treatise on charity in First Corinthians with the words: "And now abideth faith, hope, charity, these three." (1 Corinthians 13:13.) An early revelation received by Joseph Smith states, "And faith, hope, charity and love, with an eye single to the glory of God, qualify him [or her] for the work." (D&C 4:5.) Moroni in the Book of Mormon explained, "Wherefore, there must be faith; and if there must be faith there must also be hope; and if there must be hope there must also be charity." (Moroni 10:20.) Alma exhorted, "And see that ye have faith, hope, and charity, and then ye will always abound in good works." (Alma 7:24.)

These three good friends—faith, hope, and charity—become stronger because of their association with each other. Perhaps what is most important about them is that they exist together. The charitable woman is also the hopeful, faithful woman. Hence, when a woman loses hope, she will also lose faith and charity.

This is a major connection. I have known women who have let go of hope yet claimed to maintain faith. But it appears from the interlacing of these qualities that if we lack one, we shall soon lack the others. Let us cling to our faith, our hope, our charity, remembering that upon this trio hangs our well-being, now and forever.

*Second: Without hope we despair.* As pointed out earlier, Moroni wrote that "if ye have no hope ye must needs be in despair." He then added, "and despair cometh because of iniquity." (Moroni 10:22.) It seems clear that when hope leaves us, despair ensues. And despair is no better an alternative than iniquity. The woman living close to God rebounds from despair; in righteousness lies resilience.

Several years ago I watched a woman experience a brief, unhappy marriage. At age thirty-two, after many years of longing for marriage and children, she finally did marry in the temple. She discovered on her honeymoon that this man for whom she had faithfully prepared all her life had not faithfully prepared for her. He wanted the appearance of marriage, but he had no intention of living its realities. What he had said before marriage was not what he intended to do afterwards. On their honeymoon he divulged that he had only chosen her because she seemed strong and self-sufficient—able to provide for herself financially and emotionally.

She was devastated. She despaired. She wondered if her whole heart had been crushed irreparably, along with her girlhood dreams. The world was black, and everything went poorly for many months.

But a remarkable thing happened. She was still very much alive; she just didn't know it for a time. During this period of intense difficulty I watched the law of hope take its course. My friend desired righteousness all the while she struggled with choices, questions, and personal pain. Her hopeful desire, often unexpressed during those many months, worked in her. In her fertile soul dormant seeds of hope, which she had forgotten she'd planted, began to sprout. Then they began to grow. She felt them and, as she was able, nurtured those volunteer tendrils.

It wasn't easy, but hope, faith, and charity are powerful. Once growing, they are not easily dissuaded—if the soil is right. Those tendrils strengthened. Ever so gradually her anger, disappointment, pain, and even despair were replaced by fresh, fragrant plants of compassion, understanding, patience, and faith, hope, and charity. My friend lived the biblical teaching that "[she] that ploweth should plow in hope; and that [she] that thresheth in hope should be partaker of [her] hope." (1 Corinthians 9:10.)

It is undeniable that life can bring each of us heartache, devastation, and despair. It is undeniable that the gospel brings us hope, which, when well planted, grows into a magnificent garden.

In 1991 I visited Ricks College for Women's Week. There I met Aja, a beautiful, self-assured woman. She was receiving the Woman of the Year Award.

7

I was impressed by her maturity and positive comments about her own future. When I commented on this to one of the leaders, she explained that Aja had won those feelings out of a real struggle. Aja, her twin sister, and their mother had been abandoned many years earlier by her father. Aja's mother had raised the sisters close to each other and to the Church. Tragically, her mother died when Aja was just sixteen years old. The twins were not only orphaned, they were left financially destitute. They lived with friends, worked hard, scrimped, and now four years later Aja stood there on the brink of graduation and marriage. That is a story about the resilience of hope well planted and well cultivated.

*Third: Hope is an anchor to the soul.* Hebrews 6:18–19 says: "We might have a strong consolation, who have fled for refuge to lay hold upon the hope set before us: Which hope we have as an anchor of the soul, both sure and stedfast."

Little in life is sure. I became particularly conscious of this fact during the Mideast crisis, for our son Dave was serving in Saudi Arabia. During the most intense part of the conflict, including the bombing raids and the entire ground war, I was traveling in the Pacific. I was anxious for news, but found it was hard to get. When I could I studied newspapers while I was waiting for airplanes, but TV and radio news was almost inaccessible. I learned as I stood up to speak in Brisbane, Australia, that the ground war had started. I learned of the cease-fire as I left for a meeting in Papeete, Tahiti.

Throughout those weeks when I had no way of knowing where and how Dave was, I prayed a lot, and I prayed hard. Dave was always on my mind, and I longed for his well-being and for that of his wife and baby. I wondered many times each day if he was all right. It was a frightening few weeks for me.

What anchored me during that time was my hope. I have great hopes for Dave and great faith in him. I also know how sensible and spiritual his wife is. I felt good about them and their spiritual preparation for such a time. Most of all, I felt good about our mutual faith in the gospel. I knew that each member of our family, whether in Salt Lake or Boston or Walnut Creek or Riyadh or Brisbane, would pray, would expect the best, would prepare for the worst, and would live each day with hope.

Hope is a steadying influence, isn't it? As an anchor it can keep us from drifting aimlessly or getting caught in whirlpools or running into sandbars. Hope, the anchor, is essential in this world full of tidal waves. Sometimes those waves slap us from behind; sometimes we see them coming but cannot stop them or get out of the way. In all cases hope ties us to safety. The waves come and go in their fury or playfulness, but hope is always there if we will but use this sure anchor. (By the way, my son Dave is safe and well and returned in late spring of 1991 to his family.)

## How to Obtain Hope

How can we obtain hope? In all our circumstances, we can benefit from answering this question.

First and foremost, we look to Christ with joyous expectation. As Paul began his first epistle to Timothy, he identified himself in this wonderful way, "Paul, an apostle of Jesus Christ by the commandment of God our Saviour, and Lord Jesus Christ, which is our hope." (1 Timothy 1:1.) Truly, the Lord Jesus Christ is our hope. And what type of hope should we have? "A lively hope." (1 Peter 1:3.)

I was truly complimented when an Australian stake Relief Society president said, "Sister Jack, you're real." I couldn't have been more pleased, especially since this wonderful sister wanted things to be so perfect for my visit that she bought new hose because she was concerned I would disapprove of a snagged pair.

I am real—and realistic. I know faith and hope are not a placebo meant to placate the questions and desires of our hearts. They are realities. My hope and my joy in life are based upon the atonement of our Savior and the restoration of the gospel in these days. I base my life on these truths; therefore, I have reason for my hope.

Our Savior lives, and he loves us. This gospel is one of light and joy, warmth and belonging. Just consider these confirming evidences:

The angel declared at our Savior's birth, "I bring you good tidings of great joy, which shall be to all people." (Luke 2:10.) The prophets describe our Lord as he who "inviteth . . . all to come unto him and partake of his goodness; and he denieth none that come unto him, black and white, bond and free, male and female; and he remembereth the heathen; and all are alike unto God." (2 Nephi 26:33.) The Savior introduced himself as "Jesus Christ . . . the light and the life of the world." (3 Nephi 11:10–11.) Our joy, our hope begins and ends in our Savior.

A letter I received from a woman named Susan illustrates this hope in Christ:

> Not long ago I was feeling sorry for myself. . . . I've been struggling . . . to pay bills.
>
> Upon retiring to bed one night feeling the worst for the daily battle, I lay in my bed moaning to myself. . . . It was then that I looked up to the picture of the Savior I have on my wall, and I felt his eyes come to life. They seemed to look

into my very soul, and at the same time these words came to my mind: "I am here. I've always been by your side, taking the pain you feel as well. I drank the bitter cup for you and I gladly did so. I love you. I always will and I'll always be here with you every step of the way."

As tears streamed down my face, I felt like the Savior's arms had circled my body and were hugging me. I felt so secure, so loved and wanted—a feeling I can still feel as I write this on paper. The feeling of loneliness left me immediately.

As I read this letter I thought, how blessed Susan was to have a personal knowledge of the Savior. What could be more joyous?

Don't defer hope. Proverbs 13:12 states, "Hope deferred maketh the heart sick." Physically, emotionally, and spiritually, hope deferred sickens our hearts. To prevent illness, grab onto and hold onto your hope.

I love the 128th section of the Doctrine and Covenants. I ask you, as Joseph Smith asked the Church in 1842, "And again, what do we hear? Glad tidings from Cumorah! Moroni, an angel from heaven, declaring the fulfilment of the prophets... the voice of God... at sundry times, and in divers places through all the travels and tribulations of this Church of Jesus Christ of Latter-day Saints!... giving us consolation by holding forth that which is to come, confirming our hope!" (D&C 128:20–21.)

We need to confirm our hope each day. You may feel troubled, I know. Perhaps the source of your concern is your perception of how the Church is run. You may be troubled to your core by the injustices of the world. You may wonder why so many undeserving people live in abundance while so many innocents suffer. Or you may be among the innocents, bearing emotional scars because of the abuse of others. Chances are that you carry a personal problem that weighs on your soul even as you sleep. May I gently speak to your heart — don't defer hope even when you feel most hopeless. Confirm your hope every way you can.

The friend I mentioned earlier who found herself so unhappily married told me that it was the smallest things that kept her going during those first weeks when all her world looked black. A bunch of crocus burst through the snow, then announced their victory with purple blooms. The robins whistled from their nest in her front-yard tree. The sun broke over the horizon every morning. People in her office lived their quiet routines. A person spoke kindly to her at the grocery store. Her little niece hugged her around the legs. Each small, loving, daily detail confirmed her hope. They showed that life still was good. She didn't feel it, but she did not defer her hope. She focused instead on every confirmation that God lives. And if God lived, life could still be sweet, and she could feel hope again.

## What to Hope For

What should we hope for? One of our chief hopes, in this life, is for a better world. We express this hope for a better world by investing in it now.

Our investment of hope is measured in the sum of small things. My neighbor Amy planted a spring garden every year of her adult life. Her own failing health did not dampen her need to plant the flowers she knew she might not live to see. Every mother invests daily. One mother I know pinned a note on her two-year-old each morning that said, "Don't give up. I will turn three." Now, that's hope!

I admire people who read to the blind or take a neighbor to the store, those who organize a neighborhood crime watch or local recycling program or tree planting in the park. I admire people who hug each family member daily or remember their aunts' birthdays, those who take neighbors' children with them on trips, and those who can be silly with their friends. I know a widow confined to a wheelchair who crochets dishcloths for all her Relief Society sisters. She takes great personal interest in their homes, children, and all their concerns. She asks her visiting teachers to deliver her gifts at church to the sisters celebrating their birthdays. All our efforts in the home, the workplace, and the community are investments in a better world. The prophet Ether taught: "Whoso believeth in God might with surety hope for a better world, yea, even a place at the right hand of God, which hope cometh of faith, maketh an anchor to the souls of men [and women], which would make them sure and steadfast, always abounding in good works, being led to glorify God." (Ether 12:4.)

Just think of all the small ways you live with hope for your world. Each day you take a vitamin with iron, you're planning for the future. Every time you spring clean, you probably say, "Whew, I'm glad that's over. I won't have to do it for a year." You bottle fruit so there will be cherry pie next winter. You pore over the atlas, studying the roads you'll drive on your next family vacation. Whether you recognize it or not, your days are full of a hundred acts springing from your personal perfect brightness of hope.

Alfred, Lord Tennyson's poem "Ulysses" helps me understand hopeful investments in the world. You remember the story of Ulysses, the Greek hero of Homer's *Odyssey*. Through Tennyson's words we see Ulysses as an old man, still looking out to sea, still seeking the adventures of his youth. He reflects upon his increasing age, his position, his responsibilities, his experience. And having recounted them, he then says:

I am a part of all that I have met;
Yet all experience is an arch wherethrough
Gleams that untraveled world whose margin fades
Forever and forever when I move.
How dull it is to pause, to make an end,
To rust unburnished, not to shine in use! . . .
Come, my friends,
'Tis not too late to seek a newer world.
Push off, and sitting well in order smite
The sounding furrows. . . .
We are not now that strength which in old days
Moved earth and heaven, that which we are, we are—
One equal temper of heroic hearts,
Made weak by time and fate, but strong in will
To strive, to seek, to find, and not to yield.

I enjoy thinking about Tennyson's ideas, about Ulysses' hope for a fruitful future. I like the phrase "How dull it is to pause . . . to rust unburnished." I met a spry, eighty-one-year-old woman in Perth, Australia, who has been deaf since she was two. We communicated with written notes and through her own quick, descriptive hand movements. When I asked her what she loved to do most, she wrote in big letters, "Drive a car." Then she added that she didn't like to drive in Perth because it was too dull. She missed driving in Sydney where the traffic is heavy, the lanes are narrow, and the motorists drive like Evel Knievel. This woman was definitely not rusting away.

I also love the lines:

Yet all experience is an arch wherethrough
Gleams that untraveled world whose margin fades
Forever and forever when I move.

More than ever, I find my favorite archway is the one on my own front door. My home is the source of my fondest dreams and best hopes — also some of my finest adventures. What better archway to look through than the one through which I'll find the people I love best in the world?

One glorious thing about my stage in life is realizing how meaningful my investment in relationships has become. I am grateful for my relationship with the Lord. I'm glad for every moment I've spent in prayer, in study, in service. I'm grateful for every friend I've made, for my husband, for every child I've had, for every person with whom I've shared a gospel experience. And I am happy to know that those relationships can get even better. My relationships always give me hope.

The thirteenth Article of Faith reminds us, "we hope all things." I asked some of my friends and family what they hope for. Here's a short list:

My sister says, "I hope my family continues to love each other and to be good friends."

My elderly neighbor says, "I hope I'll endure independent to the end."

My son Eric says, "I hope my CPA practice will grow."

I say, "I hope the sisters will understand the joys of the gospel."

My single friend says, "I hope I'll get married and have a family of my own."

My physician husband says, "I hope my patients recover quickly, without complications."

My teenage neighbor says, "I hope our baseball team takes state."

My niece says, "I hope my children grow up remembering a happy home in which they felt secure."

We do hope all things, don't we? How much happier our lives are when we daily add the conscious optimism of hope. Emily Dickinson wrote:

"Hope" is the thing with feathers—
That perches in the soul—
And sings the tune without the words—
And never stops—at all—

I think of hope as a basket full of glorious spring flowers, each blossom representing one part of what my family, my friends, and I hope for. Together these hopes are a radiant, abundant, fragrant bouquet. Whatever our metaphor for it, hope remains an effervescent, expectant, happy part of life.

# *Charity*

I suppose that when the Relief Society general president talks about charity, an image of a woman carrying a loaf of homemade bread to a neighbor comes to mind. You may even have thought of two visiting teachers bringing a casserole to a new mother, or visualized women serving in the welfare canneries of the Church. These are stereotypes I don't mind at all because they are images of women giving.

But I want to expand your view of Relief Society and your definition of charity. Charity is all those acts of service, but it is more. It is a condition of the heart.

I hope you won't think of charity as guilt-imposing "musts," but as the quality correctly defined in the scripture as the pure love of Christ — something personally validating and glorious and peaceful and joyful too. It is all of those things to me.

Charity is one quality worth developing because it endures always. "But charity is the pure love of Christ, and it endureth forever; and whoso is found possessed of it at the last day, it shall be well with [her]." (Moroni 7:47.)

Charity is a critical quality — an essential, bedrock part of our lives. But how we develop and exercise it varies as much as each life does from another.

In February 1991 I was in Australia and visited with several sisters in their homes. One sister in Sydney, Marilyn Jones, proudly showed us a picture of her handicapped son, age sixteen, and told us how hard she had worked for eight years to get a neighborhood recreation facility for her son and other children with handicaps. She had to get zoning changes, private funding, volunteers, play equipment, and government grants, but she finally was successful. When we arrived she had just returned from the facility, where she is now employed a few hours a week. She said, "I think I liked it even better when I wasn't paid."

I marvelled at her persistence. She had looked at her life and figured out what she could do. I thought of Moroni 7:45, "Charity suffereth long, and is kind." There is much more about charity in this scripture, but that phrase struck me. I'd like to share some of my thoughts about it.

Have you ever wondered what it means to say "charity suffereth long"? It doesn't mean that charity is a painful process. To "suffer" in this context means to wait patiently, to tolerate, to hold out, to allow. Charity is patient; it doesn't give up on others. However, I do not equate "long-suffering" or "patient" charity with submissiveness to others or lack of energy. Just the opposite— charity is energetically persistent in reaching its goals. It is submissive only to the Spirit of the Lord.

Sometimes the most important thing we do for others is to suffer long in their behalf. An English teacher helps a fourteen-year-old boy through Shakespeare's "Romeo and Juliet"; a father takes on the Boy Scout troop; a woman serves as president of a Primary of 250 children; a grandmother helps her grandson learn to ride a bike; an employer teaches a new staff member in the midst of the busiest season of the year. In these and hundreds of such cases we have opportunity to "suffer long."

This is the suffering that works understanding. It reminds us that others have been patient with us, that the process of individual growth means we take turns suffering long and being suffered for.

Charity is also kind. That word *kind* suggests the simple actions, the tender way of speaking, the gentle touch — all of those effective ways of influencing others, which we can do as a habit every day when we have developed the charitable way of thinking.

Think about the little things that can bring joy to people's lives. My sister is one who does such things for me. When I'm crunched she'll look for a blouse, or leave some soup and bread at the back door when I've been away, or entertain at her house when we have guests. Those little actions become big blessings.

So are the words we say. At risk of sounding unrealistic and Pollyannaish, I think we can always find something kind to say if we try. Joseph Smith taught: "Nothing is so much calculated to lead people to forsake sin as to take them by the hand, and watch over them with tenderness. When persons manifest the least kindness and love to me, O what power it has over my mind." (*Teachings of the Prophet Joseph Smith*, comp. Joseph Fielding Smith [Salt Lake City: Deseret Book, 1976], p. 240.)

When my sons were sixteen years old they were a challenge to me. Mary Ellen Edmunds shared an idea that might have helped me through that trying time. She suggested that parents could try complimenting their adolescents honestly like this: "Son, you breathe really well. I like the way that you breathe, in and out, in and out, so regularly and nice." In most cases, we can find something honestly kind to say. Charity really is the sum of all these small acts of kindness.

Perhaps one of the most renowned givers of charity, Mother Teresa in India, has said, "We wait impatiently for the paradise where God is, but we have it in our power to be in paradise with Him, right now; being happy with Him means:

> To love as He loves,
> To help as He helps,
> To give as He gives,
> To serve as He serves."

> ( *Love, A Fruit Always in Season,* Dorothy S. Hunt, ed. [San Francisco: Ignatius Press, 1987], p. 110.)

We have our own Mother Teresas who translate that concept into real life. There is no publicity when you share, week by week, the same blessings of kindness in your own way. I have a dear friend in my neighborhood who brings me flowers every week of the spring and summer—as long as there is anything in bloom. She leaves them on the front porch or at the back door, and sometimes I get a cheerful note or an interesting excerpt from her journal with them. I took inside the first daffodils and tulips of spring, and left the big tub of magnolias and apricot blossoms on the porch so the neighbors could enjoy them also.

Another friend, Sharon, wondered what she could do to comfort a neighbor whose son had been killed in a motorcycle accident. The neighbor was not an active church member and Sharon was anxious to help but didn't know what to do. She offered a prayer that she could bring some solace, and went without anything in her hands. In her visit she felt impressed to bear her testimony of the Atonement and the opportunity to live with a loving Heavenly

Father. That assurance was just what the neighbor needed. She said, "I have prayed to know where my son was. Nobody has ever told me. That's what I needed to hear."

Being kind is nothing more than reaching out with gentleness and understanding. How desperately that is needed in this brash, coarse, insensitive world! Kindness suggests offering help without demanding something in return, being able to sense others' needs.

Modern Latter-day Saint women remind me of exemplary women from the scriptures. I think, for example, of Rebekah, the wife of Isaac and mother of Jacob and Esau. Rebekah's great experience started because she was charitable when she met a stranger and his caravan at the well.

Rebekah was kind to the servant of Abraham. Without knowing him, she politely drew water for the thirsty traveler and also for his camels. She led him to her brother's house and, when she introduced him, discovered that he was the servant of her uncle. Rebekah learned that he was on an epoch-making errand to find a wife for his master's son Isaac. Her drawing of water was the sign prompted by God. What a happy reunion and rich reward followed for her, because of an act of kindness.

This story tells us something about our own acts of charity. The chance to serve came while Rebekah was at work watering livestock, a normal task for a young woman of her country. She observed a need. Respectfully, she offered an act of service—and a new world of relationships opened.

We too will find opportunities for charitable service all around us in the course of our days' activities. We need to be observant of needs. And we will find that our acts of kindness open wonderful friendships.

One of the greatest examples of charity I know was shown by some

Latter-day Saints in Choteau, Montana, who rallied to help my young friend Robin after a disastrous car accident in which her sister and nephew were killed. She was seriously injured herself, and on arrival at the hospital in their town she asked for an LDS bishop to give her a blessing. After the branch learned of her condition there wasn't a moment when a Relief Society sister wasn't sitting with Robin, ready to give comfort and help. The whole branch came to see her off at the medical evacuation flight, brought a corsage, and sent her cards after she returned to Calgary. Six months later, Robin and her new husband stopped in Choteau on their honeymoon to go to church and thank those Saints. I think charity is most effective when it springs from within, naturally and cheerfully. That is why we talk about developing and exercising charity.

Lynanne wrote a letter from Denver to my counselor Chieko Okazaki describing her charitable career:

> Currently I am tutoring a little girl in reading twice a week. . . . She is in the second grade and was held back once. She can barely read on a first-grade level independently. So I felt compelled to help. Her mother is a single mom who runs a day-care business in order to be at the crossroads for her family the best she can. I do get paid . . . slowly. But that's okay. I only hope I can help the little girl. When she goes off track for the summer I am going to meet with her everyday because I think she needs daily help. (Letter to Chieko Okazaki, May 10, 1990.)

Our service varies according to the seasons of our lives. At each age there are different strengths and opportunities. We can't do everything all the time, but if our hearts are right we don't need to feel guilty. My daughter-in-law Jill, age twenty-six, served as a counselor in Relief Society with a president age seventy-eight. Jill encouraged taking casseroles to new mothers because she could see that need. The older president was alert to the challenges of illness and living alone. All viewpoints are useful.

We find many excuses not to reach out to others. Most of us are occupied with our personal responsibilities. We are afraid we may interfere in others' lives. It's sometimes more comfortable right where we are—far away from the suffering. Yet when we act, rewards come to us and to others. Sometimes we may reach out physically to *do*. Other times we can be most charitable if we *don't*. For example, refusing to make or join in speculative, critical, or irresponsible public comments is a great act of charity.

I hope that we will catch the vision that, although Christ's teachings are not always convenient to fulfill, the blessings of charity allow us to really know joy. The Lord loves women. He is mindful of each one of us. He simply asks us to do what we can and do it lovingly. This is confirmed in Revelation 2:19: "I know thy works, and charity, and service, and faith, and thy patience, and thy works; and the last to be more than the first." To me this scripture says that we add to our works the personal qualities of charity, service, faith, and patience. We do what we can. Then our works will be more enduring; they will be an evidence of our pure love of Christ.

# *Sharing the Joy*

s most Latter-day Saints do, I always conclude my prayers "in the name of Jesus Christ," but often I conclude them "in the name of our Savior, Jesus Christ." When I say these words I visualize Jesus in the Garden of Gethsemane, seated beside a large rock, hands folded before him, pleading with the Father. The scriptures describe it like this:

"And he was withdrawn from them about a stone's cast, and kneeled down, and prayed,

"Saying, Father, if thou be willing, remove this cup from me: nevertheless not my will, but thine, be done.

"And there appeared an angel unto him from heaven, strengthening him.

"And being in an agony he prayed more earnestly: and his sweat was as it were great drops of blood falling down to the ground." (Luke 22:41–44.)

## *Joy in the Savior*

The word *Savior* and the thought of the Atonement stir such feelings of gratitude and awe that I can hardly express them, but whenever we sing "I

Stand All Amazed," it rekindles those feelings. I love that hymn but am so touched by the words that I can hardly sing it for tears:

> That he should extend his great love unto such as I,
> Sufficient to own, to redeem, and to justify.
> Oh, it is wonderful that he should care for me
> Enough to die for me!
> Oh, it is wonderful, wonderful to me!
> (*Hymns,* no. 193.)

Shortly before Jesus was crucified he met with his disciples. He didn't have a long time to be with them. Some of his final words to them were:

"And ye now therefore have sorrow: but I will see you again, and your heart shall rejoice, and your joy no man taketh from you.

"And in that day ye shall ask me nothing. Verily, verily, I say unto you, Whatsoever ye shall ask the Father in my name, he will give it you.

"Hitherto have ye asked nothing in my name: ask, and ye shall receive, that your joy may be full." (John 16:22–24.)

How can our joy be full? Joy comes from what we receive when we ask the Father in the name of Jesus Christ. Our joy may be full as we accept the Savior and his teachings, as we pattern our lives after his example. We cannot do this by merely reading the scriptures about him. We must actually experience the situations he encountered, react in the way he did: by not judging, by loving the sinner, by serving when it is not convenient. Our Relief Society motto "Charity Never Faileth," encompasses this kind of action. We give charitable, Christlike service because we have accepted his teachings.

The people of Alma in the Book of Mosiah understood the joy that comes through accepting the Savior. In fact, they jumped for joy at what they received. Alma had gathered a group of people together and was about to baptize them. He carefully explained the covenant they were about to make, wanting to be sure they understood:

"And now, as ye are desirous to come into the fold of God, and to be called his people, and are willing to bear one another's burdens, that they may be light;

"Yea, and are willing to mourn with those that mourn; yea, and comfort those that stand in need of comfort, and to stand as witnesses of God at all times and in all things, and in all places that ye may be in, even until death, that ye may be redeemed of God, and be numbered with those of the first resurrection, that ye may have eternal life—

"Now I say unto you, if this be the desire of your hearts, what have you against being baptized in the name of the Lord, as a witness before him that ye have entered into a covenant with him, that ye will serve him and keep his commandments, that he may pour out his Spirit more abundantly upon you?

"And now when the people had heard these words, they clapped their hands for joy, and exclaimed: This is the desire of our hearts." (Mosiah 18:8–11.)

If you have had any experience with missionary work you can imagine Alma's joy at having been able to share with this group that which had brought him so much happiness and peace.

One of my favorite books of scripture is Third Nephi. I think of the glorious experience of having the Savior descend after the crucifixion in Jerusalem, saying to the multitude, "I am Jesus Christ, whom the prophets testified shall come into the world." (3 Nephi 11:10.) I try to comprehend the words that evoked verses fifteen through twenty-one in the seventeenth chapter. When Jesus realized that the multitude could not bring themselves to leave him, he was filled with compassion, and he blessed the sick and afflicted, gathered the little children around him, and prayed to the Father. These verses give a glimpse of what he might have said, and the joy of it.

## Joy in This World

Do you think it is possible to be truly joyful and happy in the world we live in? Is it possible to enjoy life amidst all the confusion, war, sadness, and corruption? When was the last time you "jumped for joy"?

Joy is the easiest of emotions to experience when everything is going right. But there are also hard times in life. This is an imperfect and frequently tragic world. Some of its wretchedness sooner or later is bound to break on our emotional shores. We get discouraged and feel depressed. In these times we need God's help to be joyful, positive, and constructive.

I was interested in the title of a book that was published a few years ago about the city of Calcutta, India. This city has an almost overwhelming collection of human misery. Millions live in horrendous slums. Countless thousands eke out a wretched existence on a few square feet of sidewalk. For so many who live in this city, life must be unspeakably dreadful. Yet the book is titled *City of Joy*. You see, amidst all that is so horrible and miserable, there is an extraordinary amount of love, sharing, helping, and giving among those people. Individually, the situation might be hopeless. But many have found ways to gather together and help each other. They don't deceive themselves about the misery — but they also don't magnify difficulties. In facing facts, they make the most of what they have. And they are happy! In so many ways it is a city of joy.

Let me share some things in my life that bring me joy.

1. Just thinking about joyful music brings favorite melodies to my mental ear. I love Caesar Franck's "Symphonic Variations" and Chopin's Second Piano Concerto, Faure and Brahms, Mozart and Mahler. It is hard for me to listen to some pieces as background music while I am reading or writing because the music transports me. I'm often distracted, stopping to think, "This is my favorite part!"

Some years ago I was friends with an elderly woman who was not only a talented performer on the piano but also a piano teacher. I met her when I was her visiting teacher in New York City. Back in Utah, she came to see me nearly every week and would teach me when I had time for lessons. I will ever be grateful to her for the way she expanded my mind and increased my appreciation and understanding of more-than-ordinary classical music. She died in 1986 but daily continues to share great joy with me through the fine music that I wouldn't have known but for her—and because she willed me her grand piano.

2. A source of great joy for me as a mother comes in the achievements of my family. We read in 3 John 1:4, "I have no greater joy than to hear that my children walk in truth." That is reality for me, as it would be for most mothers.

In our family February 5, 1991, was a "D-day." That was the day one of our sons got the results of his CPA exams: "Don't call me, I'll call you" day. He passed! Another son graduated from medical school a few years ago. What a joy that was! It was all the greater because of the traumatic application process he had gone through for two years. When he didn't get accepted the first year,

Dave did not permit himself to be discouraged. He took more and more classes and worked nights at the post office. Twice he was on the alternate list at two medical schools. The day his acceptance arrived almost rivaled the thrill of graduation. Since he earned his medical degree, I realize an even greater joy when I see him leaving family parties without complaining and treating his patients at all hours with compassion, sensitivity, and great skill.

Regardless of whether an achievement in my family is grand or small, it still gives me a warm inside joy. One Saturday afternoon I got an exciting telephone call from my grandson Robert in Massachusetts. "Gramma, I just called to tell you that my Pinewood Derby car won in all the regions today. I came in first in the pack, and then second in the district, and then today I won the fastest out of 250 cars in the region." That was a big "share the joy" day.

3. In another dimension of life, I feel an explosion of joy in my head when I discover a new idea or a new turn to an old concept. One day, for example, I was taken with the phrase, "the humanizing role of a museum," implying the need we have for influences that nurture the best in human feelings and express moral values. I now understand better that a museum can help us respond well to the gentle, the poignant, the noble, the faithful. Those refining feelings are important in raising our level of sensitivity and our appreciation for the humanities, the arts, the music, the realm of ideas—all those disciplines that create civilizations. If we lose these humanizing attitudes, we will have lost an important means for improving our world. That new idea has given me many happy moments of thought.

4. I thrive on new adventures. One day while we were backpacking in the Uintah mountains of Utah, I climbed over three 12,000-foot mountain passes in one day. Of course, we started at 9,000 feet—but the exhilaration of

reaching three mountaintops was awesome. It was a hot day, and I rolled up my pants. That action inspired the family joke, "My mother wears army boots." I also like a good shot on the golf course and the weightless feeling of waterskiing on a lake of glass.

In early March 1991 I was in Tahiti—a joyful visit among wonderful people. Two things about that trip stand out. One was seeing luxuriant, verdant growth and prolific blossoms everywhere, and the other was hiking in the rain up a muddy path to a tropical waterfall hundreds of feet high, supporting a huge philodendron leaf over my head for an umbrella. I find great fulfillment in the beauties of nature—fulfillment that is both physical and spiritual. The beauties of nature are some of the most compelling reasons for my belief in God, the creator of the earth and all that is in it.

5. Spiritual joy comes in many forms. Sometimes answers to prayers come instantly and immediately, even before we get up from our knees. It seems as if the Holy Spirit is waiting to respond as soon as we open ourselves to receive that influence. At other times, we labor long for answers.

When our son Gordon graduated from the University of Utah in accounting, he began looking for a full-time job. He was married, his wife was pregnant, and both had been working part-time. That situation obviously needed to change. He had been diligent in searching for work. On his last two interviews, he was told he was being considered, but no firm offer came. We knew it was time for a family fast and special blessing. About a month later he telephoned, "Can I borrow $150?" He had been invited to come to San Francisco for a job interview. It was successful. Someone asked how the firm knew to call him. Gordon answered, "They didn't. But I was sending letters and resumes to every feasible company in the yellow pages. The day my letter arrived, an employee resigned. Until that moment they didn't even know they needed a new accountant." Certainly the Lord responded to our prayers. That brought spiritual joy.

Many years ago my mother came to Boston where we were living to have an operation on her heart—a very new procedure at that time. The risks were high; the doctors explained the options and told her she had a 50 percent chance of survival. Her doctor was amazed when mother stated confidently that she was willing to take that risk. She was willing because of the priesthood blessing she had received before leaving her home in Canada, which stated: "Whether your recovery be instantaneous or over a period of time, it is a miracle." We had mother with us for seventeen years longer than we would have without the surgery. I was blessed not only to be close to my dear mother longer but also to be assured once again that the Lord hears and answers the prayers of his loving children.

6. As an experienced member of Relief Society and as a human being, I can tell you that joy comes from unselfish service. I have great admiration for the contribution of Mother Teresa. When she received the Nobel Peace Prize, she restated her philosophy that small acts of service represent godliness. In the eyes of God, humble work is great. Little acts of kindness are desperately needed.

I am also touched by the philosophy of a respected friend, Donna Lee Bowen, who says, "All the things that really matter, that determine who we are— spirituality, access to the Lord through prayer, humility, obedience, patience, and so on—are traits that are largely invisible to the outsider. It is very difficult to discern their presence unless you reach out to a person in love, and then you see them."

My first counselor, Chieko Okazaki, tells of an experience she had as a little girl in Hawaii, years before she joined the Church. Someone in their little village put together a Christmas pageant and assigned her to be an angel, and her line was: "Fear not: for, behold, I bring you good tidings of great joy." (Luke 2:10.) She was a Buddhist at the time and it was years before that little girl came to know what those good tidings of great joy meant to her personally. Do *you* know what they mean to you personally? The message is to all of us and each of us: "Fear not: for, behold, I bring you good tidings of great joy!"

I know there have been and are and will be times when we mourn and struggle, but we have reason to be joyful—to rejoice, to enjoy, to "jump for joy." I know God lives. What comfort and joy this sweet sentence gives!

# *Gratitude*

A few years ago, one of my friends who has built a cabin up Ogden Canyon was working there chopping wood. Something prompted her to go into the kitchen, where she found the heater in flames. Instinctively she picked up the heater and threw it out the door, saving the cabin. In the process one hand, which had partially shielded her head, and much of her face were severely burned.

When I called to express my sorrow at the accident, she was not bemoaning her fate. She was full of gratitude. Although she had been in a great deal of pain, she said, "It could have been so much worse. I was really blessed. I look like a prize fighter, but I was afraid I'd lost my dogs, and they were safe." In this painful and sobering experience, she was contemplating her blessings, not her losses.

President Ezra Taft Benson gave this counsel: "We need to be more grateful. I think there is no true character without gratitude. It is one of the marks of a real strong character to have a feeling of thanksgiving and gratitude for blessings. We need more of that spirit in our homes, in our daily association, in the Church, everywhere." (*God, Family, Country* [Salt Lake City: Deseret Book, 1974], p. 202.) These are the words of a prophet, as important as if Moses or Jeremiah or Samuel or Alma had said them. In fact, Alma did convey a similar message in these words: "[Ask] for whatsoever things ye stand in need, both spiritual and temporal; always returning thanks unto God for whatsoever things ye do receive." (Alma 7:23.)

I believe there is a definite link between gratitude and spirituality. To begin to feel gratitude, we first have to recognize and be aware of the blessings around us. Those who are unaware of their blessings miss the opportunity of rejoicing in the goodness of God, the richness of life, and the diversity of others. It is difficult for such people to reach out to bless others. I believe that personal peace and increased humility often follow our expressions and feelings of gratitude.

I remember one beautiful, sunny October afternoon when I had gone home early. I was setting the table in the dining room, anticipating a gathering of my family, which is always a joyful occasion to me. The red maple tree outside the window was vividly framed against a larger tree with yellow leaves tinged in green. There was a softening autumn haze in the air, and flowers were still blooming on the balcony. I thought of the words of Edna St. Vincent Millay: "O world, I cannot hold thee close enough!"

It is not difficult to give thanks for that which is good and beautiful, if we take time to notice. But what about nature when Hurricane Hugo wreaks devastation or the San Francisco earthquake destroys homes? How can we be thankful for wars or big-time operators who prey on the finances of others?

Many are familiar with the story of *The Hiding Place*, a book written about two Dutch women who were imprisoned during World War II for harboring Jewish refugees. Corrie and Betsie lived by the precepts of Christ and found comfort in reading the Bible. Their prison barracks were dimly lighted, dirty, foul-smelling, crowded, and constantly patroled by Nazi guards. Worst of all, they were plagued by fleas. But as soon as the sisters arrived, Betsie found cause to give thanks to God. First she rejoiced that she and Corrie were together. Next she praised God that no inspectors had taken away their Bible. Then she found good in the crowding because many more women would hear the word of God as they read it. But when she went on to express thanks for the fleas, her sister Corrie impatiently interrupted. That was too much. Betsie urged patience, citing Paul's counsel to the Thessalonians: "Rejoice evermore. Pray without ceasing. In every thing give thanks: for this is the will of God in Christ Jesus concerning you." (1 Thessalonians 5:16–18.) In giving thanks for *everything,* they acknowledged that even unpleasant circumstances could be a gift from God.

And so it proved to be. The fleas discouraged inspections, which in turn protected them from having their Bible confiscated. They were able to hold worship meetings and share Christ's message with their fellow prisoners. In expressing their gratitude for all things, they learned how much the Savior loved them and how mindful he was of their welfare. (Corrie ten Boom with John and Elizabeth Sherril [New York: Bantam Books, 1971], pp. 197–99.)

I suggest a mental exercise, following the example of Betsie and Corrie. Think of three things you are thankful for. Then think about three things you are definitely *not* thankful for. Give thanks daily for those three negative things as well as for the positive ones. I tried this experiment. I'm not thankful for my husband's annoying habit of chewing ice. Then again, I am thankful it's not candy. I'm thankful he has teeth in good condition. I'm thankful we have ice.

Why do this? God can use our changed attitudes to change facts. If we are unaware of his blessings, we miss the opportunity of rejoicing in the goodness of God, the richness of life, and the diversity of others.

There are many ways of expressing thanks. Perhaps each person does it in a little different way. Consider the synonyms for gratitude used by women and men in the scriptures.

Mary, the mother of Christ, pronounced a beautiful psalm of praise: "My soul doth magnify the Lord, and my spirit hath rejoiced in God my Saviour." (Luke 1:46–47.) The verb *rejoice* is found frequently in the minutes of the Female Relief Society of Nauvoo as counselors Elizabeth Whitney and Sarah Cleveland and others expressed their good feelings at uniting together in charitable works and sisterly association.

Nephi's thanks for the Redeemer rings changes on the verb *delighteth*. It is a happy word, speaking from his inner being:

"Behold, my soul delighteth in proving unto my people the truth of the coming of Christ. . . .

"And also my soul delighteth in the covenants of the Lord which he hath made to our fathers; yea, my soul delighteth in his grace, and in his justice, and power, and mercy in the great and eternal plan of deliverance from death.

"And my soul delighteth in proving unto my people that save Christ should come all men must perish." (2 Nephi 11:4–6.)

*Hallelujah* is a Hebrew word meaning "praise ye the Lord." It has been used as a shout of thanksgiving. Perhaps we should make our first words of the day and our last each night some such word of gratitude.

In my family we say, "Aren't we blessed!" to express our intensely thankful feelings. This was true the time we came home from a drive to find that the windows had been closed during a rainstorm. We use it on those occasions when the family is all together, especially for a holiday. And our son Gordy exclaimed it when his eighteen-month-old baby had finally slept through the night every night for two weeks.

When I read Alma's counsel to ask "for whatsoever things ye stand in need, both spiritual and temporal; always returning thanks unto God for whatsoever things ye do receive" (Alma 7:23), I sometimes wonder about my needs. I seem to have no problem defining my temporal needs, but I feel that I can keep my temporal needs and wants in bounds only as I define my spiritual needs. They are somehow harder to focus on. I need patience, discipline, humility, more sacrifice. I need to remember, as the saying goes, that "we are not human beings having a spiritual experience; we are spiritual beings having a human experience."

We are literally sons and daughters of a Heavenly Father who loves us, and I love him. I believe we each have divine qualities that we have to work to develop. The Spirit of the Lord can bear witness of what we must do to develop these spiritual qualities.

There is a definite link between gratitude and spirituality.

—When we are aware of our blessings, we can reach out to bless others.

—When we rejoice in the goodness of God, we find opportunity to rejoice in the richness of life and the diversity of others.

—When we express our gratitude, we feel increased humility and personal peace.

As the Lord said to Joseph Smith and the Saints in Missouri, "My friends, fear not, let your hearts be comforted; yea, rejoice evermore, and in everything give thanks." (D&C 98:1.)

# *Building Love*

**I**n August of 1990, I was in California for the blessing of our eighth grandchild. Three of our four children with their families were there, and being together with them made me realize that love was my favorite subject. It is the thing that I enjoy talking about the most, and the loving relationships that I have with my family and friends are some of my greatest blessings.

I was blessed to grow up in a small community with grandparents, aunts, uncles, and cousins all living close by. The activities of the whole town were based on the standards and programs of the Church. From these people I learned early on about the love of the Lord and the love of others.

I learned that love meant spending time together, laughing together, supporting each other, and helping each other in our work. That meant that I was trained early in life how to do laundry, how to mend, and how to clean house by a mother whose standards of cleanliness were very high. I was often sent down the street to help my grandparents with a task or errand. They were special friends and wonderful role models, immediately at hand.

We all enjoyed family get-togethers, especially in the summer and at Christmastime. These involved music and eating and lots of reminiscing.

Even more important than the recreation together, the love of the Lord and of the gospel of Jesus Christ pervaded all family living. In the covenants of the Church is a binding power that draws us into the circle of God's love—as individuals and as families.

As I look at the troubles in the world, I am convinced that they all stem from lack of genuine love for one another. When love is displaced by greed, hatred, or desire for power, people suffer. We begin to solve problems by building love in our own intimate circle, in our families.

What is a family? In a society where traditional families headed by father and mother with children at home are almost a minority, we need to enlarge our definition of *family* to include single people, couples alone, single-parent families (both male and female), blended families, part-member families, divorced families, families with foster children, grandmothers raising grand-children, and sometimes extended families living together.

In all of these families there are joys and there are stresses. How do we learn about healthy family relationships? Where does the support come from? In my growing up near many relatives, it was aunts and uncles and grandparents who provided the role models. Relatives supported each other when new babies came, or the workload was particularly heavy. We were involved in each other's family processes. As President Gordon B. Hinckley has wisely counseled, "We need each other—sisters, husbands, sons, daughters. We need parents, brothers and grandparents. We are woven together in a tapestry of love, tears, laughter, frustration and joy." (Regional Representatives Seminar, April 1, 1988.)

For those of us without extended family members nearby, these relationship blessings must be provided by others. Brothers and sisters in the Church can sustain us. Relief Society can strengthen families, every kind of family. It must.

As Norma B. Ashton suggests, "The young mother who feels that the days of diapers and dishes will never end, the single woman trying to find her niche, the middle-aged woman with wrinkles and arthritis starting to appear, and the older woman who wonders where she fits in, all need to ask, 'What does this situation require of me?' Then we can choose a course of action and pray for strength and faith to find the joy promised to us wherever we find ourselves on the path of life." (*Women of Wisdom and Knowledge*, ed. Marie Cornwall and Susan Howe [Salt Lake City: Deseret Book, 1990], p. 22.)

Let me share three ideas that will help us build love for one another in our homes:

1. *Share your best times with your family and make your family the source of your best times.* Family life is rigorous. I found this out again most recently when I went to tend four little children while their mother was in the hospital having the fifth.

We had a full schedule, gathering together school books and homework papers and lunch money before the school bus came in the morning for two of them. Then I turned my attention to the preschoolers, pushing Doug and Marianne in the tire swing and letting them play with neighborhood children. Doug went off for half-day school, and I put Marianne down for a nap. With the return of the school bus came a demand for snacks — in fact, I think I prepared fifteen snacks each day plus treats for after supper. We ended the evening unitedly working on a solve-the-mystery book and laughing over each other's antics on a video. There was joy in that association, but I was reminded that serving a family requires ingenuity and endurance. It is not the easiest or the simplest or the least demanding way to live, but it is a most rewarding way.

Early in our marriage Joe and I decided that family was our first priority and that we would demonstrate this by making our time together meaningful and pleasant. Working together as a family is important to me, even though sometimes that brings stressful moments (for example, when we were encouraging our sons to finish their assigned yard work or their newspaper deliveries).

As a family we took up hobbies, not realizing that they would be such bonds of family togetherness as they have turned out to be. Our idea of the world's greatest family vacation has always been to go skiing or golfing together. Earlier years included backpacking and a shared enjoyment of wilderness areas. Now that we have a new generation of Jacks coming along, naturally they are learning the same sports that we have come to love so much.

When we've played together we have learned about each other. We have enjoyed each other's company and have shared family jokes. We have developed healthy competition and good relationships. I have seen our sons each learn golfing and skiing from their father, and I have seen them pass him up although he is still in competition because he is steady. After nine holes the constant cry is "What's the score?" The scorekeeper says, "Dad's one up on strokes and you're two up on holes."

Things of the world, business concerns, friends, and other pressures can pull family members apart, but if we find things that we can enjoy together and in which everyone can participate, even though each has an individual life, we can form lasting bonds. My husband has made time for his sons, who know that they are every bit as important as his profession. The work ethic of many men demands full time for career, sometimes at the expense of family. But an awareness of the importance of family life on the part of both mother and father can build love in a way that nothing else can.

*2. Talk about the gospel every day.* When I am focusing on the gospel of Jesus Christ my life becomes more centered on his teachings. I realize that I am most loving when I am conscious of how he would have me conduct the affairs of my life. I am happiest when I feel that I am doing as my Heavenly Father would want me to do.

I take regular early-morning walks with a good friend. We have been neighbors for many years and walking companions many mornings in the spring, summer, and fall—and even in the winter when it is not too icy. During these many years of walking we have had great talks about our growing families and now mature and married children and grandchildren. We don't consciously decide to talk about the gospel, but I realize that our conversations are based on the desire we have to serve the Lord and to help our children live the gospel. It has been wonderful for me to have someone I could talk to about my feelings for the Church and the questions that I have in my own attempts to progress.

There were years when several women from our ward congregated at 7:00 A.M. on the corner to walk together. In fact, the mailman labeled us "The hiking honeys of Holladay." One summer my neighbor Joye wanted to join us but she had a new baby and couldn't. One day she telephoned me and said, "On your walk tomorrow stop by my mailbox." When we did, we found a note written on a piece of lined school paper. It was her "gospel lesson from the mailbox." Usually a scripture with a question or a bit of wisdom to ponder, this discussion topic led us daily to share our insights and to encourage and enlighten each other. At the end of the summer, we compiled these notes into a booklet called "Notes from the Mailbox" by Joye Billings.

I wish I could say that my family had wonderful success in morning scripture reading. We haven't done it consistently, but there were a couple of years when we were pretty faithful and we completed the Book of Mormon and the Doctrine and Covenants. I have to admit we didn't have stimulating, sparkling discussions on the meanings of the scriptures in the early morning with our young boys, but we did do the reading together, and it oriented us as a family to receiving guidance and direction from the scriptures.

Many people view "Dear Abby" as a source of wisdom, and if you operate your life according to her advice, you can't go too far wrong—according to public opinion. But even though Abigail Van Buren is a woman of great common sense and even compassion, her advice column is not a source of celestial counsel. There is a difference between measuring behavior by today's standards of decency and using the measure of eternal truth. We learn eternal truths by learning more about the gospel every day.

A few years ago I realized that as much as I loved such children's books as *Alexander and the Terrible, Horrible, No Good, Very Bad Day* and *There's a Monster in My Closet*, there was something more enlightening I could do for my grandchildren, even though they were far away. So I purchased some tapes and recorded stories from the Bible to send to them. In such ways I can reinforce with my grandchildren how important the gospel is to me.

I find that as my husband and I talk daily about individual scriptures or concepts in lessons, it draws us closer together. Sometimes I miss the things he reads and emphasizes, so from listening to him, I gain new insight. He is especially good at using the study guides and background information to enrich our scripture reading.

I enjoy my grown sons and their wives with whom I can also share the gospel. I watched one daughter-in-law, who had graduated from Brigham Young University, expand her perspective as she moved to North Carolina. She was entering a world of discovery. At first she talked about the strange ways of the South; then that feeling evolved to "I feel sorry for people who have never lived any place but Utah." I saw her listen to different points of view and exercise wisdom and tolerance toward others. When she moved to New York she was instrumental in organizing a playground volunteer system for the apartment building in which she lived. Watching Judean reach out so personally and so energetically to others has taught me a great deal about important gospel principles of love and service.

*3. Express love often to your Heavenly Father, to your family, and to friends.* Expressions of love should be shared daily, not just saved for special occasions. It is good to express love verbally. We shouldn't take for granted that our loved ones already know how we feel; we need to say it.

My friend Carol Clark opens each of her prayers with the words, "Heavenly Father, we love thee." She has learned the value of expressing her love for God at every opportunity.

An elderly friend who was a stroke victim lost his facility of speech. He is having to relearn the facial and vocal motions necessary to produce sounds. During this tedious process, he wrote in his notebook, "I need to speak to tell everyone how much they mean to me." That is a lesson for all of us. Often as I look out my kitchen window at the beautiful mountains, the colorful trees that I see there, I tell the Lord how grateful I am for the eyes he has given me, for my love of his beauties, for my knowledge of the gospel, and for my membership in his church.

To summarize—these have been my suggestions for increasing love:

1. Share your best times with your family. Work and play together. Put family before business and friends and other pressures.

2. Talk about the gospel daily. Study scriptures and live gospel values.

3. Express love to your Heavenly Father, to your family, to your friends, every day.

In the last few years Church leaders have dedicated several new temples. Any event of this character calls for personal rededication. So said President Spencer W. Kimball and his counselors, writing to priesthood leaders before the dedication of the Jordan River Temple. They urged stake presidents and bishops to call upon all members to prepare their hearts and minds for this historic event: "Use this occasion as an opportunity to cleanse their lives of anything displeasing to the Lord, eliminating from their hearts any ill feelings and feelings of envy or enmity and seeking forgiveness for anything that is amiss in their lives." (First Presidency Letter, September 28, 1981.) These barriers to love must be overcome.

If the troubles in the world stem from lack of genuine love for one another, the simple yet profound commandments given by the Savior are the answer. The greatest commandments deal with relationships: "Love one another, as I have loved you." (John 15:12.) Our loving interaction with others — with family, friends, business associates — will heal the world. Such interactions call for more understanding among us and increased ability to communicate. We all can strive to improve our sensitivity in relationships. Love begins in families, families in all their dimensions. The bottom line is that we care about each other and are willing to show it.

# *Discovering the Power of the Word*

One word that especially intrigues me is *discover*. It means much more than merely to find, implying to find for oneself, to arrive at through search or discovery. It has aspects of a child playing hide-and-go-seek at grandmother's house: "I dis-covered him" in the attic or the clothes closet. The concept of discovery has changed and continues to change the world. Some things can be discovered over and over as various individuals find for themselves a new idea, a new world, a new concept.

As I thought about discovery, I thought about the power of the word. Words have been the means of great discovery for me. I grew up in a small town in southern Alberta. In our small Mormon community at the edge of the prairie there were no paved roads, lots of mud and dust, one movie theater, and several gas stations. Many of the men worked with their hands. Grease and mud were always on my father's clothes when he came home at night. Nearly everyone in town had a barn and a garden. People there worked hard and modern conveniences were few. However, despite those harsh conditions, manners and grammar and education and cleanliness were important to my mother.

Poor grammar did not exist in our home, although "I seen" and "we was" were heard elsewhere. When I would go through the teenage "There's-nothing-to-do-around-here" routine, Mother would reply, "Well, dear, why don't you read. Have you read Eliot's *Silas Marner* or Hawthorne's *The Scarlet Letter?*"

What I learned from my mother was that we actively sought refinement in every circumstance. It was part of being a Latter-day Saint. Refinement was part of our lifestyle. This meant that words were used correctly and explored through fine literature.

In his interesting book, *The 100: A Ranking of the Most Influential Persons in History,* author Michael Hart lists Ts'ai Lun as number seven in his ranking. Ts'ai Lun was the praised inventor of paper. An official in the Chinese imperial court about A.D. 105, he is seldom mentioned in history texts, yet what a legacy he left. Hart lists Johann Gutenberg, the inventor of printing, as number eight. He developed the utilization of moveable type and the printing press in such a way that a large variety of written material could be printed with speed and accuracy. You remember the Gutenberg Bible. Hart makes the point that Ts'ai Lun's invention complemented Gutenberg's, one incomplete without the other. (New York: Carol Publishing Group, 1978, pp. 66, 72.)

What matters is that with paper, information becomes generally accessible. Our modern problem, though, is too much paper. We are concerned about shredding documents, about recycling the accumulations of newspapers and photocopies and junk mail that inundate our homes and offices. We are assaulted by a barrage of words, so that we may have lost the glorious simplicity of the right word. Like so many good things, the power of a single word is often buried in a plethora of meaningless verbiage. Think of the power of simple words exchanged in a marriage ceremony, a compliment, a covenant, a sincere expression of affection.

Poets know the value of the right word. Consider this poem, "Circles," by Carol L. Clark:

The circles of their influence never cease.
Women of an earlier time
Gently ply the heart of our living,
As water waves distantly begun mutely lap a far shore —
Permanently marking.

Though storms of earthly loss battered
Their bastioned souls and
Unutterable sorrow swept away the
Joy of birth,
They endured.
Anchored, yet buoyantly swelling with love
Beyond themselves.

From the life of Enoch the prophet, we learn about the word. Moses 7:13 recounts: "The rivers of water were turned out of their course; and the roar of the lions was heard out of the wilderness; and all nations feared greatly, so powerful was the word of Enoch, and so great was the power of the language which God had given him."

I heard President Hinckley comment after a French-speaking dedicatory session at the Toronto Temple, "I have discovered that language is beautiful when it is used to express the love of God and his Son Jesus Christ and the eternal gospel which has come to us through the revelations to Joseph Smith."

In Oliver Cowdery's description of the heavenly visitation of John the Baptist to restore the Aaronic Priesthood, he said in part, "While the world was racked and distracted . . . our eyes beheld — our ears heard. . . . Then his [the angel's] voice, though mild, pierced to the center, and his words, 'I am thy fellow-servant,' dispelled every fear." (Joseph Smith, *History of the Church of Jesus Christ of Latter-day Saints* [Salt Lake City: Deseret Book, 1951], p. 43, footnote.)

The power of the word. It can change the course of rivers, refresh our souls, dispel fear. Think of experiences you have had with words that have touched your life. There are some words I avoid, like *burden* and *stereotype*. There are others that touch my soul, like *hallelujah*.

Insights from ancient and modern prophets speak to me of the many uses of words. Let's go back to some words given as commandments — as opposed to suggestions or ideas or thoughts. When the Lord gave the Ten Commandments, he said to Moses: "Write thou these words: for after the tenor of these words I have made a covenant with thee and with Israel." (Exodus 34:27.) Two of those ten commandments relate specifically to words: "Thou shalt not take the name of the Lord thy God in vain," and "Neither shalt thou bear false witness against thy neighbour." (Deuteronomy 5:11, 20.)

It seems that everywhere we look in the scriptures the Lord reminds us of the power of the word — his word.

Let me share a few more ideas about the word. When the new Relief Society presidency was called, we initially spent a lot of time praying, thinking, and talking about our goals and desires for our sisters. We remembered Joseph Smith's seventh lecture on faith. The opening question in that lecture is, "What are we to understand by a man's working by faith?" Answer: "We understand that when a man works by faith he works by mental exertion instead of by physical force." The significance for us was that we had to use mental exertion — thought and the words to express it — in order to move forward.

We considered these thoughts:

God *said*, "Let there be light;" and there was light.

Joshua *spake* and the sun stood still.

Elijah *commanded* and there was no rain.

The Savior said, "If ye have faith as a grain of mustard seed, ye shall *say* to this mountain, Remove . . . and it shall remove." (Matthew 17:20.)

The righteous power of a word.

We chose a refocusing of our mission based on words that are powerful, motivating, and concise:

*Build* personal testimony.

*Bless* the individual woman.

*Develop* and *exercise* charity.

*Strengthen* families.

*Enjoy* a unified sisterhood.

To me this is compelling.

In our training we always suggest that sisters must base their actions upon gospel principles, derived from scripture. Again, the power of the word of God underlies what we do.

In thinking of the power of words, I remember President Spencer W. Kimball's address at the general women's meeting in 1978 when he said, "We should be . . . concerned with the woman's capacity to communicate. . . . Good women are articulate as well as affectionate." (*Ensign,* November 1978, p. 104.)

The dictionary defines *articulate* this way: "able to speak; expressing oneself readily, clearly, or effectively." President Kimball addressed the topic again in the 1979 women's meeting: "Much of the major growth that is coming to the Church in the last days will come because many of the good women of the world . . . will be drawn into the Church in large numbers. This will happen to the degree that the women of the Church reflect righteousness and articulateness in their lives and to the degree that the women of the Church are seen as distinct and different—in happy ways—from the women of the world." (*Ensign,* November 1979, pp. 103–4.)

Perhaps my greatest concern about the education of women throughout the world is that without the power of the word, women cannot deal with the best of ideas. Without the ideas—the ability to "work by mental exertion," as Joseph Smith said—women cannot improve their positions or those of their families.

The power of the word is remarkable. The blessing to discover it is great indeed. The way is open. There have never been greater opportunities to discover and learn—whether formally, in a classroom, informally from each other, or, most powerfully, from the Lord.

# Strengthening Families

When you hear the word *family*, what do you picture? What does a family look like? How does it feel?

I'll tell you what family looks like to me. To me family means the people I love the best, the ones who can cause me the greatest concern, the ones who bring me the greatest joys, the ones I laugh the most with, pray the most about, miss the most when they're gone. Family is a tremendous source of happiness to me.

You will note that I did not say that family relationships are always easy or pleasant or satisfying. It's hard work to create a good marriage, to raise children and make a home. But in that process of creating a family, some of the most extraordinary events of life can occur.

In the world of each of our homes, our families have the most remarkable capacity to bring us joy, humor, spiritual insights, work, and more types of challenges than we could enumerate. I enjoy reading family cartoons in the newspaper. In a recent one the mom walks into the living room saying, "What is it now?" Her daughter complains, "Ditto is telling Trixie a secret and he won't tell me." Mom's response: "No more whispering and no more teasing, OK?" Ditto says, "OK, does that mean we can go back to screaming and fighting?"

Families are like that, aren't they? Sometimes as parents we think the choices are obvious; our family members remind us there are many ways to look at the world.

Perhaps this is why our Heavenly Father made such a point of identifying us as part of his family. Have you ever considered how many times the men and women in the scriptures are identified in terms of their place in the Lord's family? Or how many times we are likewise named as sons and daughters of God? Let me share a few examples.

Our Heavenly Father said to Moses, "Behold, I am the Lord God Almighty . . . and, behold, thou art my son." (Moses 1:3–4.)

Matthew began his account of our Lord's ministry by calling it "the book of the generation of Jesus Christ, the son of David, the son of Abraham." (Matthew 1:1.) It was critical to place the Savior in terms of his earthly father's lineage before Matthew could share the account of the Savior's heavenly lineage.

President Spencer W. Kimball said, "The family is the basic unit of the kingdom of God on earth. The Church can be no healthier than its families. No government can long endure without strong families." (*Ensign*, May 1978, p. 45.) This prophetic statement deserves our closest attention, for it is true. I often think of President Kimball's words in personal terms: My ward is no stronger than my family. My neighborhood is no stronger than my family. Our son served a mission in Taiwan and often quotes Confucius's saying: "Strengthen oneself; build the family; govern the nation; peace under all the heavens." To me this means if we control ourselves and build our families, the nation will be governed, the world will be ordered, and all under the heavens will be peaceful.

President Kimball also told us over a decade ago that "the time will come when only those who believe deeply and actively in the family will be able to preserve their families in the midst of the gathering evil around us." (*Ensign*, November 1980, p. 4.) I admire my friend Lois, who told her adult children: "Our speaker in sacrament meeting suggested that each of us should develop a passion for something righteous. You, my children, are my passion. I am passionately interested in your welfare, spiritual and temporal, and I will continue to passionately pray and work for your welfare." Imagine the effect such a statement had on those children, now raising families of their own.

President Ezra Taft Benson has given us equally potent counsel about families. He said: "If we continue with present trends, we can expect to have more emotionally disturbed young people, more divorce, more depression, and more suicide. The family is the most effective place to instill lasting values in its members. Where family life is strong and based on principles and practices of the gospel of Jesus Christ, these problems do not as readily appear." (*Ensign*, November 1982, p. 59.)

I believe this counsel from our prophets. I also know that many sisters bear the burden of family members who have turned away from the gospel or turned on each other or turned hearts inside out because of their actions or inaction. I hope they will understand what I share in the loving spirit with which I intend to convey it. I speak from my heart when I say we must revere and honor the family, even when our family members bring us pain. No family is perfect, because no person is perfect. And the source of steadiness is always the Lord, who loves us all, no matter what our circumstance.

No matter what goes on in our families, we should remember that family relationships are powerful. They can grow into mighty fortresses, bringing us great strength in times of personal conflict. I'd like to share ten ways to help our families grow in the strength of the Lord.

*1. Invite the Spirit of the Lord into your home, and acknowledge it often.* When I travel I have the blessing of learning in the homes of Saints in various nations. I have found that the Spirit abides in many, many types of homes throughout this earth. What a comfort it is to enter a home and feel at home there. I always feel that way when the Spirit of the Lord is present.

As a mother introduces me to her family, I can tell something about their relationship. Very often that same mother will speak lovingly of her family when we're alone together. I know that a good mother has the Spirit of the Lord with her. I know because the "fruit of the Spirit is love." It is also "joy, peace, longsuffering, gentleness, goodness, faith, meekness, temperance." (Galatians 5:22–23.)

When those things occur in your home, point out to your family that such wonderful feelings are the fruit of the Spirit. Sometimes when children are touched by the Spirit, they may not know what they are feeling. Don't let those moments pass without gratitude and comment. When a child feels the joy of accomplishment, or you have a peaceful Sabbath, or an older sister is long-suffering with a younger one who just destroyed her new nail polish, that's the fruit of the Spirit. Invite it. Then acknowledge it in prayers, in blessings, and at other times.

*2. Talk together.* President Benson has said, "Strong families cultivate an attribute of effective communication. They talk out their problems, make plans together, and cooperate toward common objectives. Family home evening and family councils are practiced and used as effective tools toward this end." (*Ensign,* May 1984, p. 6.)

I like that idea of counseling together as a family. "Where no counsel is, the people fall" (Proverbs 11:14), states the scripture. Isaiah reminded us,

"Take counsel together." (Isaiah 8:10.) I think family councils are important for three reasons:

— They give each family member opportunity to participate with an equal voice. If you vote about a vacation spot, the three-year-old's vote has the same weight as the sixteen-year-old's.

— Each family member becomes responsible for the decisions and feels part of the process of making them.

— Each family member feels part of a family entity and acknowledges family relationships as being important.

A family council is effective in many types of families. These councils work for families with father, mother, and children at home. But they work equally well for family members who no longer live together, for a single parent and children, or for roommates. They work because they are based upon mutual respect, good communication, and the desire to develop meaningful relationships. Since we are sons and daughters of our Heavenly Father, we need to invite him to participate in our deliberations too, by praying together before and after these meetings.

Joe and I referred to the family council portion of our weekly home evening as "family business." It has always been a favorite part of home evening. Everyone was so anxious to get to family business that it was hard sometimes to concentrate on the lesson. I loved having each family member unfold his plans and needs for the week. We used to talk about who would get the car when, what kinds of food the boys wanted me to buy, and on and on. It was a weekly highlight for us all.

I still rely on my son Bill as one of my best sounding boards. When I am working on a talk or some other major project, I often call him and talk it through with him. This pattern of reliance on his good judgment began in our family councils many years ago. Bill lives across the country now, but because of the relationship we built, in part through family councils, we communicate very effectively with a fax machine and a telephone. Bill blesses my life in many ways, especially as we continue to counsel together.

3. *Use humor.* Paul wisely stated, "A little leaven leaveneth the whole lump." (Galatians 5:9.) What is the leaven you use when things start sagging at your house? I have found that humor is a superior leaven in most circumstances.

A family I know well consists of a widowed mother and two grown children. They tell me their best humor comes when they kneel together in preparation for their nightly prayer. They circle a huge, overstuffed Queen Anne chair which they call the prayer chair. Kneeling there together, they often begin to tell funny stories about what has happened during the day. Pretty soon they're laughing and carrying on. This custom brings the day to a positive close and prepares them to thank the Lord and seek his blessing through prayer. They go to bed with lightened hearts and a happier perspective.

My counselor Chieko Okazaki plays the ukulele and tells us regularly to "Lighten up!" It's very good advice.

4. *Develop family traditions.* My family's traditions are a blend of what my husband and I brought to our marriage and what we've developed with our children. Whenever we traveled, we read and sang in the car. We love to sing together, even though no one in the Jack or Low clans is headed for the Metropolitan Opera. When I was young, my father and my uncle used to sing together at each family event. My twin cousins served missions in New Zealand, and now they do Maori war dances at our reunions. Because of our family heritage, we celebrate a Swedish Christmas Eve, which is great fun.

I grew up with lots of family reunions, and they remain one of my favorite events of the year. One summer I asked my grandson James, who was twelve, to keep our journal of the reunion. It was his job to see that everyone participated in writing something for our family record. I cannot claim that the journal worked too well, but at least James knows that keeping a record matters to me.

A sacred family tradition is the giving of blessings on important occasions. Joe is never more eloquent than when he gives one of the family members a father's blessing. Before our oldest son, Dave, left for Saudi Arabia to serve with the Desert Storm troops, he asked Joe for a blessing. Dave then gave a blessing to his wife, Gayle, and to their daughter, Charlotte. These blessings were sustaining for all of us.

If you wonder if you have any family traditions, ask your family sometime. You may be surprised what traditions they remember from the times you have all been together.

5. *Show commitment.* Nothing is more important than building a sense of identity and belonging in a family unit. My friend tells me that when she was a teenager, as she left with her friends, her mother always said to her, "Remember who you are and what you stand for." My mother said something just about like that, only she added, "Do you have a clean handkerchief, dear?" To suggest that family members remember who they are means that they do, in fact, know who they are in the first place.

I believe that one major reason many people get themselves in trouble is that they do not know who they are. They don't stand for anything. I suggest you consider setting some standards that identify your family. Family mottos are one way to create a sense of identity. Another is to create a family crest.

That's what we have done. Our crest has representations of the blending of the American and Canadian cultures. These two emblems join to portray our Scottish heritage. The treble clef symbol depicts our common love of music and harmony within the family. Wheat reminds us of the law of the harvest and of the fertile plains of southern Alberta, Canada. The temple reminds us we are a covenant family, eternally linked together.

The importance of the sense of identity shown in our family crest does not lessen over time. In fact, I've learned that I am drawn to my roots now more than ever. I have reached the age where I understand Erma Bombeck's story about putting on a sweater and watching her mother's arm come out the sleeve. My niece who just lost her mother a year ago wrote to me, "I still think about my Mom and miss her every day. Especially now that I see myself doing so many of the things she did in her young married life. I'm even starting to say things to Hailey that she said to me. Now I just hope I can be the kind of mother she was." My family identity truly affects me and all I do.

*6. Acknowledge mentors, role models, and others significant in your family members' lives.* I have been grateful almost from the day our first son was born that my children have such excellent models. Uncles, aunts, cousins, neighbors, Primary teachers, Scout leaders, and friends have blessed us all.

I think of a schoolteacher who made the effort to find us while we were on a family vacation to Disneyland. She had just learned of a scholarship she thought our son would have a good chance of getting. The application was due while we were gone, so she went to the effort of finding us. How grateful we all were for her efforts.

My friend Doral visited one day when our youngest son was about fourteen years old. He wasn't happy with anything or anyone and I felt very frustrated about his attitude. Doral said, "Just love him." It was exactly what I needed to hear. Carol Clark was an interested "big sister" who helped my two youngest sons get through high school English.

As a parent and grandparent, I feel very blessed that so many good people have helped my family. My grandparents lived two houses away from me while I was growing up. I live two thousand miles away from my grandchildren. Who will help them? I grandmother the Jensen children next door, and I am grateful for those in Massachusetts who take an interest in my grandchildren.

7. *Work together.* My sons always knew we did the work first so we could play. Joe and I decided we would institute this policy early, so our boys knew that was how it was in the Jack household. Sometimes our sons wanted to debate with us about the relative merits of work and an important baseball game. But they knew the policy, and that helped all of us. I used to play Sousa marches on the piano when I wanted them to get up and get busy on a Saturday morning. It didn't do much for them, but it helped me get going.

A friend talks about her father's idea of work. There was one way to do a job—his. And that meant to do it well. And there was one best use for holidays: family work parties. She recalls painting the house on Labor Day for many years. (Her father relished Labor Day because they could observe it so literally.) Everyone would have an assigned area to paint, and Dad would come around to comment on the work. If the painters didn't measure up to his expectation he told them, and then showed them how to do it properly.

Behind their dad's back, the brothers and sisters vowed they would never subject their children to such tough work, especially on holidays. Now, married and parents themselves, every one of them works on holidays and to the exacting standard they learned from their father.

There is more than one kind of work. President Benson has told us, "Every family has problems and challenges. But successful families try to work together toward solutions instead of resorting to criticism and contention." (*Ensign,* May 1984, p. 6.) Working through problems and working on relationships can be demanding for all of us. But this work is a lot more important than painting the house. Relationships are the essence of this life, after all. The gospel of Jesus Christ is based on laws governing our relationships with the Lord and with each other. We must never subordinate our work on relationships to other kinds of work.

*8. Play together.* Our family has played together a lot. We played games for home evenings and on Sunday nights and every Christmas holiday. These games honed our skills and generated a lot of competitive spirit, sometimes too much. There have been games that ended in fights, but the overall spirit has been one of fun.

I play lots of games with my grandchildren now when I have a chance. I have to admit that playing five straight games of Candyland is a bit tedious, but I never weary of that relaxed, fun time with my family.

*9. Pray together.* President Benson says that successful families "pray for each other, discuss, and give encouragement. Occasionally these families fast together in support of one of the family members." (Ibid.) Children learn much more than the form of prayer when they participate with adults in prayer. They learn the spirit of prayer, the purposes of prayer, and the fruits of it. As President Benson counseled, "Prayer is the means to acknowledge appreciation for blessings and to humbly recognize dependence on Almighty God for strength, sustenance, and support." (Ibid., p. 7.)

Joe prays with great meaning, and I think our boys learned a lot about the power of the priesthood they bear from listening to their father pray and give blessings over the years. I have a strong testimony of the blessing of fasting and praying together as a family. It works.

*10. Learn together.* We must teach our children so they understand about faith, repentance, baptism, and the gift of the Holy Ghost. A young mother recently told me about her three-year-old daughter. It seems that Grandma wanted to read the little girl a story, but she wanted to play. She said, "Grandma, I read at night." Her mother reads to her every night before bed. They read lots of Book of Mormon stories as well as *Winnie the Pooh* and other favorites.

Learning together does not always involve parents teaching children. When I typed my sons' high school and college papers, I learned many things. Bill's paper on holography and Dave's on the Bible provided two of my best moments of learning.

We used to take short family trips to local places like Golden Spike Monument and ghost towns in Utah. These were wonderful mini-adventures and great learning experiences as well.

Throughout this chapter I have written a lot about my family because it's the one I know best. My family isn't perfect. I have only told you the good parts — and as I remember them. Let me share with you a son's version: "She experimented with paying us to memorize worthy literary quotations, tried to instill responsibility and growth with job charts, and, with Dad, struggled to have regular family home evenings. Each attempt succeeded to a degree, but I don't remember many parts of my childhood which would qualify for the perfect parenting examples found in the back of the *Ensign* magazine."

Be that as it may, the principles discussed are sound. As you go over these ten points, you can adapt them to your own family circumstances. We can be — and must be — united in bringing comfort, love, and peace to each person and hence to each family. My vision of Relief Society is a glorious one, for the Lord has given us the opportunity and the means of becoming a force for good greater than any before seen among women in the history of the world. Let us joyfully engage in the work of strengthening families.

"We Being Many Are One"

# These Things
## Are Real

I have wanted for thirty years to meet the woman against whom more Latter-day Saint women have compared themselves than any other woman in the Church. She's often thought of as "Superwoman." Some call her the typical Relief Society sister, the woman who makes fabulous bread, plays the organ like a professional, and dresses her impeccably groomed children in the clothes she has made.

Where is she? Who is she? What does she do that makes her seem beyond the reach of any woman? I've made a careful study and I have found this woman. In this chapter I'll introduce you to our sister so we can see her as she is.

The prophet Jacob taught, "The Spirit speaketh the truth and lieth not. Wherefore, it speaketh of things as they really are, and of things as they really will be; wherefore, these things are manifested unto us plainly, for the salvation of our souls." (Jacob 4:13.)

I wish to speak of "things as they really are, and of things as they really will be." For many of us, comparing ourselves to a practically perfect Latter-day Saint woman is part of how things are. While some of us are motivated and encouraged by such imagined or real-life models, others are disheartened and discouraged by this same ideal woman—whether she is a composite of many women, or someone of whom we have read, or even someone we know.

As women make these comparisons, I hear such comments as: "When they talk about being a good mother in Relief Society, I always feel so guilty because sometimes I shout at my children." "I'm not comfortable in church because my husband isn't active." "I wish I didn't have to work, but I need a paycheck to sustain my family."

I've heard: "I'm not a mother. I'm not married and I'm most painfully aware of this in Relief Society and sacrament meeting. I often go home feeling that they don't know what to do with me in the Church."

These statements and others like them come, I believe, from unrealistic comparisons we make against some ideal. These comparisons may keep us from achieving our potential and basking in associations that will enrich our lives and the lives of others. Sometimes the basis for these incorrect comparisons comes from other Relief Society sisters, the Relief Society organization, or expectations about roles in life. Whatever the origin, the point of comparison is wrong unless it accounts for things as they really are, now and forever.

The prophet Jacob said that things as they "really are" and "really will be" are "manifested unto us plainly, for the salvation of our souls." How are these things manifested unto us? Through the fulness of the gospel of Jesus Christ, through the example of our Savior's life. Only by living his gospel can we find what is real. We can never accurately take the measure of our lives based on social, economic, ethnic, age, marital, or physical conditions. Ask yourself, are the comparisons you may make of yourself and others based on the model of the Savior's life, or do they come from trying to fit your life into the pattern of others' lives?

Sometimes comparisons creep up on us. We sit in Relief Society surrounded by our neighbors and friends, all of whom seem to raise the best children, to teach the most profound lessons, and to possess the greatest spirituality. It can feel quite discouraging.

You may say, "I'm just average. There's nothing special about me or my life." And yet it is manifested plainly to me that you are extraordinary, you whose average day is lived in accordance with our Heavenly Father's laws.

No greater heroine lives in today's world than the woman who is quietly doing her part. Generally unsung, you live everywhere—you live in Nebraska or Puerto Rico or Ghana or Canada or Czechoslovakia. You show your love for the Lord daily as you support your husband, nurture children, care for parents, benefit neighbors, serve in your school, sit on your community council, and do much of the work of this world in and out of the home. No one is more impressive than you.

I promised to introduce you to the typical Relief Society sister.

The good news is that she actually does exist.

The better news is that she is wonderful.

The best news is that she's you! And this is who you really are!

You and your three million sisters live in 135 countries and territories across the globe from Invercargill to Edmonton, from Chicago to Singapore.

Eight thousand of you are single, full-time missionaries; seventeen hundred are serving as part of a couple.

You are raising 1.2 million children plus another million teenagers.

You made approximately four million visits to each other doing visiting teaching in the year 1990.

If I could have the desire of my heart for you, it would be that you feel valued for your own goodness. The starting point is knowing that you are a daughter of God. The Young Women say together each week, "We are daughters of our Heavenly Father who loves us, and we love him. We will stand as witnesses of God at all times and in all things, and in all places." (See Mosiah 18:9.)

The Primary children sing, "I belong to The Church of Jesus Christ of Latter-day Saints. I know who I am, I know God's plan, I'll follow him in faith." When my grandchildren and their parents sing this song together with great enthusiasm, it brings tears of joy. I know who I am, I know God's plan, and this knowledge makes all the difference.

We Relief Society sisters follow our motto, Charity Never Faileth. This motto is very personal to me. It means that we love our Heavenly Father, and we best express that love through all that we do for others.

To rejoice in being a daughter of God, to know God's plan, and to follow the Savior's example of service—these things are real.

The Savior taught the Samaritan woman at Jacob's well: "Whosoever drinketh of the water that I shall give him shall never thirst; but the water that I shall give him shall be in him a well of water springing up into everlasting life. The woman saith unto him, Sir, give me this water, that I thirst not." (John 4:14–15.)

A Relief Society sister in Ghana visits a woman who thirsts for truth but cannot read. To give her sister the opportunity to drink deeply of gospel truths, the visiting teacher tries to be with her as often as possible. She reads the scriptures to her sister and explains their meaning in her native tongue.

A remarkable, peppy, saintly, sixty-year-old woman lives among a handful of Saints in Czechoslovakia. She remained active in the Church during the forty-year slumber when her country was denied full religious opportunity. This sister shares the gospel's living water as she takes an eighty-three-year-old branch president for a walk each day and does his shopping for him. He requires two canes for walking, and shopping in Czechoslovakia is no small task.

Through their daily acts of service, these women partake of and pass on to others the water springing up into eternal life.

Another woman wrote "I love being a mother. I love teaching my children the gospel. I substituted in Relief Society one week and got to give the lesson on family scripture study. This is something close to my heart, something I can't imagine family life without. After the lesson, a sister came up to me and said, 'I can't believe all you do. I don't have the patience.' But she sings and takes piano lessons. At times I've envied people who could sing well or play an instrument, because I love music.

"After my conversation with her I felt that although I had not been blessed with great musical ability, Heavenly Father had blessed me with a love of motherhood and that this indeed was a gift and a talent for which I am grateful."

Isn't the point of these three examples that each of these sisters serves as she is able, according to the needs around her? Isn't that the point of your life?

Look at all you do. You make quilts for orphans and visit women in prison. You change countless diapers and kiss away endless tears. You collect clothing for earthquake victims. You tutor underachieving children. In the Church you preside, teach, counsel, visit teach, and render countless other acts of service. You may serve as Relief Society president, or librarian, or Star A teacher, or Gospel Doctrine instructor. All that you do blesses children, youth, women, and men in every unit of the Church.

Our focus in Relief Society for this new decade reflects our quest for things that are real and for the salvation of our souls. Our mission reflects our love and admiration for you. We want you to live a life of spiritual maturity and fulfillment, free from unrealistic comparisons.

Our goal is for you to enjoy the process of life. Build your own personal testimony and rejoice with me in being a typical Relief Society woman. These things are real — testimony, individuality, charity, families, sisterhood. These are real, and so are you. I pay tribute to you.

# *Them and Us*

Once upon a time in a ward you know, a visitor attended on an average Sunday. It was a happy, pleasant ward, with great diversity. Children, youth, and adults of many ages sat together in sacrament meeting. The building seemed well kept, the leaders well organized, the lessons well taught. The visitor thought, "What lucky people live in this ward. What a warm, inviting place this must be. They must truly love one another." She decided to come again, not to look but to listen to what these people said about their relationships.

This is what she heard the next Sunday.

One Relief Society counselor said to the other, "I've decided our singles bring their problems on themselves. We reach out to them, but they don't respond. Sometimes I wish we didn't have so many in our ward."

One Young Adult asked another, "Don't you just hate Relief Society? It is always so boring. The women are all old and they only talk about married women's stuff."

A grandmother said to her friend, "I hear they're reorganizing the Primary. I hope they don't call us. We've raised our families. It's the young mothers' turn to work in Primary."

The Laurel advisor told the Beehive advisor, "Since I have been in

Young Women, I feel Relief Society ignores me. They've forgotten those of us who aren't in class every Sunday."

A recently returned missionary complained to his friend, "The girls in this ward are the worst. Why do they expect me to attend Young Adult activities in this stake when the female population is so bad?"

The Primary president said to her counselor, "I wish they would quit stealing our best teachers. We just get them trained, and the bishop gives them another calling."

An elder who taught the Gospel Doctrine class told the Sunday School president, "These manuals are awful. What is wrong with the people at Church headquarters? Just because some areas of the world are new to the gospel doesn't mean the rest of us should be stuck with these outlines."

A visiting teacher commented to her friend, "I can't believe the new district they gave me. Two of the women are my friends, and I feel silly giving them a spiritual message. I don't even know the rest of my district, so I really feel stupid trying to give a spiritual thought to these strangers."

The Relief Society president said to the bishop, "We work so hard, and the sisters just don't appreciate it. They don't seem interested. They don't even seem to care. I don't feel the sisterhood in Relief Society I used to feel."

The visitor left the ward feeling downhearted. "Why?" she mused. "Why do these fine people label each other? Why do I hear so much talk of 'them and us' and so little 'my sister and my brother'? Why do they miss the joy of loving one another?"

As you may have guessed, I am that visitor, and I have asked those questions many times after hearing all those comments in wards I have visited. Happily, in those same wards I've heard and seen much love and rejoicing in the restored gospel. I always return home thanking our Heavenly Father for the good people who populate this earth. But to my dismay the "them-and-us" mentality is alive and well, pervasive and limiting.

This way of thinking and talking about each other hurts my soul. I'm concerned about the divisiveness it creates. I'm concerned that too often we Saints inadvertently label others in our ward families as "them," somehow not like "us." Let me share an example of how some of us lapse into "them-and-us" talk without even realizing it.

Recently I visited with Relief Society leaders who have many single women in their stake. The Relief Society president began our conversation by saying, "Sister Jack, our single women are a real problem for us." What I noticed immediately was the labeling of all single women as a problem. But this good president did not realize what she had said. She continued, "I feel our singles bring many of their problems on themselves."

I asked, "Have you talked with any of your sisters who are single about their problems?"

She said, "Well, no. Not formally. But the ward presidents bring me reports, and I never feel very warm or good when I speak to them. I don't think they want to speak with me."

"When have you spoken to these single sisters? Are any of them your friends?" I queried.

"Not really. I do speak to singles at stake conference or at a stake leadership meeting. But, as I said, that's always so unsatisfying," she responded.

I asked further, "Have you invited any of the singles in leadership positions to discuss their points of view in your meetings so all the sisters might get better acquainted with them?"

"I have never thought of doing anything like that," she responded.

Do you get the point? This very conscientious president does not know the single sisters in her stake as individuals. It's no wonder she calls these sisters "them." Not one of them is her friend. Not one has been asked to participate in a meeting.

Please consider this point for a moment. Think about an experience you've had when your first impression of someone changed dramatically after you got acquainted. Maybe you couldn't stand your spouse when you first met. Perhaps your bishop has become one of your favorite people now that you've served together. In some cases roommates don't start off well—even missionary companions can be a pain on occasion. Yet, sharing experience and conversation can improve the whole world, can't it?

The Savior told us directly, "If ye are not one ye are not mine." (D&C 38:27.) There are some people in the world who I consider to be great souls. In every case these sons and daughters of God value the individual. They make it a point to get to know people—to be "one" with them. Not surprisingly, these great women and men tend to avoid making judgments about others, or putting them in categories by religion, race, gender, marital status, or age. I think both elements—loving others and judging gently—are suggested by the Savior's direction to us. When we do love others, we can become one. When we become one, we can be in the Savior's fold. It sounds simple, though I know well it can be hard to do. But it can be done.

For me, one of the most instructive stories in the Book of Mormon is that of Alma the Younger's mission to the Zoramites. The scripture records:

"Alma . . . received tidings that the Zoramites were perverting the ways of the Lord, . . . his heart again began to sicken because of the iniquity of the people. . . .

"And now, as the preaching of the word had a great tendency to lead the people to do that which was just—yea, it had had more powerful effect upon the minds of the people than the sword, or anything else, which had happened unto them—therefore Alma thought it was expedient that they should try the virtue of the word of God. . . .

"When they [Alma and his missionary brethren] had come into the land, behold, to their astonishment they found that the Zoramites had built synagogues, and that they did gather themselves together on one day of the week, . . . and they did worship after a manner which Alma and his brethren had never beheld; . . .

"Whosoever desired to worship must go forth and stand upon the top thereof, and stretch forth his hands towards heaven, and cry with a loud voice, saying: . . .

"Holy God, we believe that thou hast separated us from our brethren; and we do not believe in the tradition of our brethren . . . but we believe that thou hast elected us to be thy holy children; and also thou hast made it known unto us that there shall be no Christ. . . .

"And thou hast elected us that we shall be saved, whilst all around us are elected to be cast by thy wrath down to hell; for the which holiness, O God, we thank thee; and we also thank thee that thou hast elected us, that we may not be led away after the foolish traditions of our brethren, which doth bind them down to a belief of Christ."

Alma responded: "Behold, O God, they cry unto thee, and yet their hearts are swallowed up in their pride. Behold, O God, they cry unto thee with their mouths, while they are puffed up, even to greatness, with the vain things of the world. . . . How long wilt thou suffer that such wickedness and infidelity shall be among this people?" (Alma 31:1–30.)

Two things strike me about this Rameumptom story. First, the Zoramites' prayer was a complete perversion of the Lord's most central teachings about love. These Zoramites repeated over and over their disbelief in our Savior while they extolled their superiority over their neighbors. It is significant that those two apostate concepts appeared together: they claimed no belief in the Savior and they claimed to be apart from and better than those around them.

Second, Alma was intensely concerned about his Zoramite brethren. He prayed, "O Lord, my heart is exceedingly sorrowful; wilt thou comfort my soul in Christ." (Alma 31:31.) Alma brought them the best medicine available to cure their spiritual illness. He brought the word of God.

One of the reasons I am always so distressed when I hear the Saints talk about "our problems with singles" or "the irresponsible youth of the Church" or "the difficulties with the aged" is that all such comments reflect a distance from the word of God. "Them and us" talk like this distances us from each other too.

The Zoramites perverted correct worship by designing "a place for standing" in the "center of their synagogue." (Alma 31:13.) While we would never purposely create such a pulpit, do we inadvertently mount a form of that Rameumptom when we speak of "them and us," as if such artificial designations were in keeping with the Lord's teachings? Do we ignore the word of God by judging each other when we don't even know each other?

When we travel as a Relief Society general board, we commonly hold focus groups — informal gatherings that allow us to hear from our sisters throughout the world. We generally sit in a circle and let our sisters tell us what is on their minds and in their hearts. One of our single general board members recently reported the following episode. A sister about the same age as our board member said, "These single women. I am convinced they simply do not want the responsibilities of children. They don't get married because they take all their satisfaction from a paycheck."

I know well what is in the heart of this board member. No one could want a husband and family more than she. She went up to the sister after the meeting and said, "On behalf of the single women of the Church, I want you to know I'd do anything to have your two children, and I do not take satisfaction from my paycheck." Giving no response, the other sister turned away and started talking to someone else. My single friend was wounded and angry. She fumed, "Elaine, what our sister said was so untrue. She must never have talked to a single woman if she thinks that. Why do we make false accusations about each other?"

It's a good question, isn't it? In fact, it's a lot like Alma's question about the "wickedness and infidelity" of the Zoramites. My friend asked the kind of question each of us might profitably ask when pained by obvious insensitivity and unkindness. Why do we do things like that? I believe that as members of the Church we do not intend to hurt each other. Generally our forays into "them-and-us" talk and action come because of poor vision.

In some cases we simply are blind to the feelings of brothers and sisters close to us because we do not share their experience. A woman recently wrote me: "As a single adult I feel I have been forgotten. Perhaps you are thinking that I should be more faithful, that by trusting in the Lord I will overcome this feeling of being left out and not being cared about. Deep down inside there is a need in me that is not being filled. When I have spoken with those in leadership positions I am . . . forgotten as soon as I have left the room because they are at a loss. I don't think it is intentional. I think they are in a quandary."

Sometimes when we're in a quandary, when we don't know what to say or do, we turn away. Often that is the most hurtful thing we can do. A friend of mine says, "Disagree with me. Speak to me curtly. But don't ignore me." I feel the same way. When I talk with someone else, I can learn. I won't always fully understand. I may not always completely agree. But I will always learn. We need to learn from each other by opening our eyes to other perspectives and people.

Sometimes "them and us" occurs because we lose sight of how good we really are. Then we may climb a step or two up that ladder to the Rameump-tom, thinking we'll have a better vista, hence, a clearer view. Instead we may create even greater distance between ourselves and our neighbors. One of the reasons the tragedy of the homeless Kurdish people was so gripping is that we all saw pictures of the faces of individuals. Those men, women, and children are human beings, our fellow travelers on earth. We feel for each of them as we witness their plight. Think about the difference in your reactions to photos taken from the air of the troops dropping food to those people versus the photos taken at ground level of individuals struggling to reach that food.

I think the difference is that opportunity to look eye to eye at another person. When we step up the Rameumptom ladder, we lose that blessed chance to look at one person and see who she or he is. There are challenges to such personal interaction. It can be uncomfortable to be so "up close and personal." In certain cases we just don't see eye to eye or even hear ear to ear with members of our families, let alone members of our wards. And, of course, everywhere are people who challenge us — sometimes verbally, sometimes emotionally. The temptation to look away can be great when we disagree or feel hurt or don't like what someone says to us. Yet the Savior, who loves and understands each of us, teaches, "Look unto me, and be ye saved." (Isaiah 45:22.)

Another reason we lapse into "them and us" is that we may get a little disoriented and look in the wrong direction. The prophet Jacob explained that much of the trouble that came to the Jews was the result of looking at the wrong target. He wrote, "Wherefore, because of their blindness, which blindness came by looking beyond the mark, they must needs fall." (Jacob 4:14.) Moses set a fiery serpent upon a pole that the children of Israel who had been bitten by serpents might look upon it and live. The solution was so simple. All they had to do was look in the right direction, but not all of them did. (Numbers 21:8.)

This looking and seeing is critical. We can lose spiritual clarity in our vision in lots of ways. Whether we are blind to some experiences and feelings of others, forget how good we are, or look beyond the mark, we are missing the big picture—and no hike up to a Rameumptom erected in honor of "them and us" will refocus our spiritual lenses.

Remember what the Zoramites said when they climbed to their place alone in the synagogue? We are different and better, and it is a foolish tradition to believe in Christ. What do we say when we start up that same ladder? Things like: "I don't have anything in common with parents of little children," or, "I know the Savior said to love everyone, but he didn't know my brother-in-law," or, "Roommates are impossible. I've never had a good one."

When we choose to pattern our lives on the Savior's, that is, to really try to love others and to see eye to eye with them, good comes. On a recent trip to Australia and Tahiti, Carol, my general board traveling companion, and I were especially careful to take luggage we could carry on the plane with us. Neither of us could think of anything worse than spending several days waiting for errant bags to catch up with us. When we arrived in Sydney, luggage in hand, we joined the Area Presidency and their wives for a lunch overlooking beautiful Sydney harbor. We returned to the car to find it had been broken into. Carol's luggage – personal belongings, training materials, books, everything – had been stolen. She was left without purse or scriptures, lipstick or even a change of shoes. All she had were the clothes on her back. We had worried about waiting two days for luggage; now Carol faced three weeks on the road in Australia without even a toothbrush.

Carol called home to cancel some credit cards and told her family that Wati Martin, the wife of Area President Douglas Martin, had offered to help us get some toiletries and clothes. Wati knew we had only an hour to shop before our first series of meetings. She whisked us to a local mall and in forty minutes Carol had some toiletries, cosmetics, and one new outfit.

When we got to the Martins' home late that night, Wati went through her own closet, picking out blouses and other items she thought Carol could use. Thanks to her, by the next morning Carol had enough clothes and sundries to get by with, as well as a useful bag in which to carry them. Carol called home the next day to report that things were much improved, and her family in Utah told her that a friend of Wati's had heard about the theft already and called them to say, "Don't worry about Carol. Wati will take care of her." Nothing could have been more correct. Wati took us under her protective, loving wing and cared for our needs, which in this case included all the basics – food, shelter, and clothing.

Can you imagine how grateful we were to Wati and Elder Martin and to the others who helped us turn a disaster into an experience of love at its best?

When I returned home from this trip I began looking through my scriptures for examples of what happens when people live according to our

Savior's teachings about love. Let me share a short series of these, so we can learn from the prophets about how truly converted people live.

Alma and Amulek "went forth preaching repentance to the people. . . .

"And as many as would hear their words, unto them they did impart the word of God, without any respect of persons, continually. . . .

"And the establishment of the church became general throughout the land, in all the region round about, among all the people of the Nephites. And there was no inequality among them." (Alma 16:13–16.)

The Lamanites who became the Anti-Nephi-Lehies "began to be a righteous people; and they did walk in the ways of the Lord." (Alma 25:14.) Ammon reported of them, "We can witness of their sincerity, because of their love towards their brethren and also towards us. . . . Has there been so great love in all the land? Behold, I say unto you, Nay, there has not, even among the Nephites. . . .

"And they were also distinguished for their zeal towards God, and also towards men; for they were perfectly honest and upright in all things." (Alma 26:31–33; 27:27.)

Alma the Elder identified his people as "ye [who] are desirous to come into the fold of God, and to be called his people, and are willing to bear one another's burdens, that they may be light." (Mosiah 18:8.)

Of the people of Alma the scripture records, "They did walk uprightly before God, imparting to one another both temporally and spiritually according to their needs and their wants." (Mosiah 18:29.)

The Lord called the people of Enoch "Zion, because they were of one heart and one mind, and dwelt in righteousness; and there was no poor among them." (Moses 7:18.)

After the Savior's visit, the people on the American continent "had all things common among them; therefore there were not rich and poor, bond and free, but they were all made free, and partakers of the heavenly gift." (4 Nephi 1:3.) Time passed, life went on, yet after one hundred more years had passed away, the scriptures tell us:

"There was no contention in the land, because of the love of God which did dwell in the hearts of the people. . . . And surely there could not be a happier people among all the people who had been created by the hand of God." (4 Nephi 1:15–16.)

Finally, let me quote more of what I mentioned earlier that the Savior said to us in this dispensation: "And let every man esteem his brother as himself, and practise virtue and holiness before me. . . . I say unto you, be one; and if ye are not one ye are not mine." (D&C 38:24, 27.)

Do you see a pattern? I do, and I am grateful for these ideas:

1. The people of God love him.

2. They love each other.

3. They are greatly changed by their love.

4. They deal justly with one another.

5. They hold all things in common.

6. They are pure in heart.

7. They live peacefully together.

We could find dozens of other scriptures that echo these messages. Having heard these words of prophets and of the Lord himself, can you see why I am so distressed when I hear or witness "them and us" in our language and treatment of one another? Simply stated, nothing is more destructive to our personal spiritual growth than these small wedges we drive between us – and sometimes into each other.

How can we clarify our vision and become one?

First, we must take off our blinders. Recently a prominent family in my neighborhood suffered a great tragedy. Their troubled teenage son committed suicide. Under the influence of drugs and alcohol, he apparently sought peace in this desperate way. His fine family felt his loss intensely. Despite an enormous level of effort and outpouring of love to this son throughout his life, his parents agonized, wondering if they'd done everything they could. His siblings probably wondered the same. Neighbors and friends, in and out of the Church, responded with love, sympathy, and support.

The family sat together at stake conference just days after this tragic experience. The main speaker, who knew of this incident, gave a long talk about the problems families get into when they spend too much time on Church duties and not enough time with each other. Some members of the congregation visibly winced as they thought of this family and how the message might affect them. Right message. Wrong time. How we wished our speaker had taken off his blinders and seen the needs of our brothers and sisters.

This same sort of thing can happen in less dramatic ways. A bishop announces that all families are invited to the ward party. A single man living alone might feel less than welcome.

A Relief Society president invites sisters and their husbands to a special homemaking event. A recent widow withers a little; a newly divorced mother withdraws.

Sometimes our blinders limit our understanding of others. At times they also limit our understanding of ourselves. Recently I visited two of my sons in California. On a Saturday night I was sitting in the car with a sleeping grandchild while they took care of some Church business. While I sat there right in front of the ward, I watched a few people walk into the building. I knew that a single adult fireside was due to begin in about forty-five minutes, so I assumed these early arrivals were in charge of the meeting. A young man walked in alone and about ten minutes later walked back out. He had his hands stuffed in his pants pockets and looked very alone. I called to him, "Hey, are you leaving before the meeting starts?"

He looked quite directly at me and responded, "Does it matter?"

"Well, yes, it does. I know you've got some guest speakers, and I think you'd enjoy hearing them," I said. I knew that two Relief Society representatives would be speaking at that meeting. I encouraged him to stay and listen to them. "Have you ever heard Sister Okazaki or Sister Clark speak?" I asked.

"No," he said, "and I won't tonight either."

My heart dropped as he walked off. How I wished he could have joined me for a few minutes so I could have learned more of him. How I wished he had felt at home.

Blinders are good for horses. They keep them looking straight ahead at the road. Blinders are not so good for people, for we must look not only at the road ahead, but also at the sky above, and into each other's eyes.

It is not hard to remove our blinders, but it does require effort. The great thing about the scriptural examples we have just seen is that they are all real, and they point us in the right direction. They tell us why taking the blinders off is so useful; they also tell us how we will know when we have been successful in our efforts to do so. Most of all, they repeat over and over this truth: Love is the greatest teacher.

When Christlike love becomes our main motivator, when we really get serious about truly demonstrating our love for the Lord, good things happen.

During this past year I have felt an increased need to learn how to love others. I have prayed many times that the Lord would help me understand the many needs and circumstances of women throughout the world. In essence, I've been praying that the Lord would help me remove any blinders. I can testify to you that my prayers have been answered. I am different than I was before I received this calling. I am different now because I see more broadly, I love more profoundly, and I feel gratitude more abundantly. The Lord has been good to me. These insights have not come instantaneously, but they have come as I have applied myself to prayerfully trying to love more and understand better. I continue to pray for greater wisdom and insight, thanking the Lord all the while for his goodness to each of us.

Second, to clarify our vision we must think and then act inclusively, not exclusively. A Ricks College student recently said to me, "You know, when President Bennion meets you on campus, he treats you like he was your home teacher instead of the president of Ricks." I cannot imagine a nicer tribute. Loving people know the art of making others feel valued, equal, loved.

Learning to think and act inclusively requires thoughtfulness and good old common sense. Elder Adam Wilcox, a missionary, wrote to his family:

> We had a zone conference tonight. It seems that some missionaries from another district have been taking the meetings a little less seriously than other people feel they should. They were openly rebuked for it, and it gave me some thoughts on the relationship we place between the gospel and people. . . . It's so easy to notice what other people do wrong and how we would do things differently. Can you imagine how different the world would be if that trend was reversed and if we all noticed the positive acts of others and set these

qualities as our goal to work for rather than comparing ourselves to the negative.

Yes, Elder Wilcox, I can imagine. In fact, in my fondest dreams we treat
each other in kind ways that heal and soothe the bruises and rebuffs of life.
This wise young elder reminds us that if we will acknowledge successes and
think of ways to bring everyone in, rather than emphasize the errors or differences that leave some out, life will be better all around.

Life ought to be a grand party with everyone sitting around the same
round table. Particularly our Church experiences together should be sources
of happiness and harmony. When we're together, we should feel we belong.
How did you feel when you arrived at the last ward party you attended? Did
you come alone? Did you dread entering the building because you didn't know
whom you could sit by? Did you come with another friend? Did you spend the
time visiting with everyone in the room? Did you leave feeling happy?

Even our casual experiences together are something to ponder. Do
we enter our chapels feeling and thinking inclusively? Do we come to the party
ready to help others feel they belong? As we spiritually prepare for our Church
assignments, do we ask the Lord to help us understand those we are called to
serve? Do we pray to love and understand our family members? our co-workers?
our neighbors? our roommates? If we think and act inclusively, love may abound
among us despite our weaknesses, mistakes, and spiritual distance from each
other.

Third, avoid offense. A friend often quotes me this truth, "He who
takes offense when no offense is intended is a fool. He who takes offense when
offense is intended is usually a fool."

The Golden Rule is a much underrated commandment, in my opinion. The Savior said on both continents on which he ministered, "All things whatsoever ye would that men should do to you, do ye even so to them, for this is the law and the prophets." (3 Nephi 14:12.) This simple injunction could make life happier for thousands. I mean it—each one of us probably deals with thousands of people annually who could be blessed if we took this commandment to heart, head, and tongue.

Now, to avoid offense we must be serious about neither giving nor taking it. We will always have to deal with thoughtless people. Sometimes our own lack of experience makes us insensitive when we intend to be otherwise. Some days we are just so busy or tired or in a hurry, we speak before we think. Unquestionably, opportunities to give and take offense are plentiful.

I suggest, however, that we never intentionally litter the lives of our associates with offenses. And we can also refuse to pick up an offense when others drop it.

I know a woman from Mexico who joined the Church, the only person in her family to do so. She subsequently went on a mission, did graduate work at Brigham Young University, and took a responsible position in government. To take this job meant a move, so off she went to a new community where she had no friends. The first week in her new, suburban, North American, family ward, she introduced herself to the bishop. He promptly responded by calling her to serve in the ward library and by assigning a husband and wife to serve as her home and visiting teachers.

Because she was so new to the ward, she felt she should have been called to serve in a position that would let her mingle with the ward members. She said nothing to the bishop, but she resented being asked to serve in such an isolated environment as the library. Weeks came and went, and she got angrier and angrier about what she felt was a real slap in the face from an insensitive bishop.

About the time she got up a good boil about her Church calling, her home/visiting teachers called. They were elderly, the husband explained. They had often come by to visit, but she was never home. He complained that he could never get her on the phone. He told her she should have bought an answering machine months ago, if she expected him to ever check on her.

He continued. His knees were bad — so were his wife's — and they would no longer climb the three flights of stairs to her apartment. If she wanted them to come, she would have to call them first.

After that phone conversation, she got up a really fine head of steam. "These Anglos," she thought. "Who do they think they are? First, they shove me in a closet at the ward, then they offend me by expecting me to meet their schedule. I'll show them. I just won't come at all." True to her word, she stopped going to church. All because well-meaning people dropped offense.

Now, she could have disposed of that offense in several ways. She could have picked up the ugly thing and thrown it in the garbage. She could have asked, "What is the intent of their actions and words?" before she heated to such a hard boil. She might have stepped over the offense, laughing at the difficulty all of us have sometimes as we try to communicate. She could have explained her needs to the bishop in the first place. She could have chosen a street-level location at which to meet the home/visiting teachers. She could have counseled with an understanding friend. She could have stomped and fumed until she was able to turn the heat off and let her feelings simmer down. She could have said, "This is my Church too and no one will drive me out of it, no matter what they do or say." She could have determined to be more understanding so she could avoid treating others the way she had been treated. She could have done a lot of things. Most of all, I wish she had never taken offense in the first place.

A friend of mine recently came to visit, looking like the loser of a twelve–round prize fight. "What is wrong?" I asked, as she burst into tears. The trouble was that one of her neighbors had lambasted her repeatedly over a matter concerning their daughters, who were best friends. It seems my friend's daughter had offended the neighbor's daughter, and the neighbor had marched right over and let my friend have it. What offended my friend was first being treated as if she were responsible for her daughter's comments and then being talked to as if she were a child herself.

My friend said, "Elaine, it's bad enough to have such an unpleasant encounter once, but she won't let it go. She's talked to me four times about the same trouble, even though the girls have forgotten the whole episode. What should I do?"

My answer: "Bob and weave."

"What do you mean?" my confused friend asked.

I suggested, "Don't take offense at this. Isn't this the same neighbor who was so angry when your son cracked her kitchen window with a baseball? He paid for the damage, but she insisted on telling you several times how distressed she was. After she'd vented her feelings, she was fine.

"Now, she apparently needs to vent when she's angry, and it seems she doesn't get it all out the first time. Just because she needs to say it more than once doesn't mean you have to stand there like a punching bag waiting for her to hit you again. Don't stand there flat-footed; keep moving.

"What do champion prizefighters do? They don't just stand in one place when someone approaches with boxing gloves on. They take some initiative, and so should you. Write her a nice note explaining your feelings. Invite her family over for a family picnic. Go shopping together. Tell her the next good joke you hear. Bake her some brownies and take them to her while they're still warm. Pour her a nice glass of milk, and when she takes that first mouthful, hurry and explain how much you'd like to be her friend. Then treat her as if she were your best friend. No matter what she does, keep moving. Do what you can, maintain a sense of humor, then let it go."

Having received this counsel from another friend when I was a young mother, I know it is sound. Take initiative, do good, enjoy humor, and, most important, avoid offense.

"Them and us" are not words the Lord uses to talk about us. He has called us his children, his friends, his sheep, his lambs. He has admonished us to be one with each other, to follow the pattern he and his Father have set for us.

The prophet Isaiah wrote, "They shall see eye to eye when the Lord shall bring again Zion." (3 Nephi 16:18.) May we work to see eye to eye; may we become one as we treat and speak of each other as the sons and daughters of God, sisters and brothers in the gospel of Jesus Christ.

# *Building Bridges*

I n a recent *Life* magazine article, author Roger Rosenblatt wrote, "So many problems of national consequence roll through the country these days, begging for a forum, a stage, a someplace where we might spread them before us and talk them through. But either the someplace does not exist, or we have no interest in looking, content or discontent to let thoughts on the most painful, complicated problems of our lives go unexpressed." ("Can We Talk?," *Life*, August 1991, p. 18.)

In my roles as wife, mother, grandmother, church worker, and community volunteer I see Mr. Rosenblatt's lament lived out much too often. I fear he is right that too many people are too busy or frightened or self-interested to talk things through. I believe that if people would get together and talk with each other in a spirit of mutual respect and caring, most problems in this world could be solved.

The nineteenth-century German poet Goethe said that the things that matter most should not be at the mercy of things that matter least. I imagine that most of us agree with that thought, but it's harder in the living than in the saying. One of the things that matters most is building bridges, that is, creating opportunities where loving discussion can take place between family members, co-workers, fellow volunteers, and others in our arena of life.

Aileen Clyde, a good friend and counselor, talks about her husband Hal's explanation of building a bridge. He says it's really the art of getting it in your head where to put the legs and then being sure both ends meet in the middle. The bridging that takes place in good communication is like that too — it requires some real sharing and thought and risking.

The first step in building a bridge of communication involves knowing ourselves and being willing to risk saying what we really feel. Only when we recognize our true present feelings are we able to learn and grow in our views.

The second step is entering into discussions where our thinking and feelings may be challenged. Superficial chat is much safer and easier — and lonely, because we are listening only to the surfaces of life. When we refuse to participate in and partake of real discussions, we abdicate responsibility for becoming informed. To reach out to other human beings, we need to listen to others and be willing to form different opinions. We need to assimilate new information, weigh it against what we already know, and decide what to keep. This is the process of education — the ongoing education that enhances life.

After planting these footings, we are ready to build the part of the bridge that links one person to another. We are ready to try to understand others' feelings and beliefs, without passing negative judgments. When my friend Anne traveled to Ireland to meet her son at the end of his mission, she visited a Relief Society homemaking meeting and was surprised, even dismayed, to find a group of women engrossed in watching a video of "The Little Mermaid." She quickly judged that these women did not comprehend the purpose of home-making meetings. The president explained, "We don't always do this. Sometimes we go bowling." Still inwardly critical, it took Anne some time to reflect that for these sisters, living long distances from each other in a politically unstable community with few luxuries in their homes and little pocket money, coming together in sisterhood to relax in a rare hour of entertainment fostered the renewal they craved. Relief Society was meeting their needs. This homemaking activity was worth the effort.

If you have ever built a new house, you know that the structure has to settle. There are creaks and groans sometimes as a house settles in. Relationships are like that—sometimes as we build true understanding, we feel a few aches.

In August of 1991 I traveled in Africa, where I learned much from listening and observing. The first black stake Relief Society president in Nigeria responded to a letter from the Relief Society general offices, "Your letter arrived and lit a candle of joy in our minds. We are mothering the first stake in Nigeria."

In our hemisphere we don't carry babies on our backs, as they do in Nigeria. While I don't understand everything about being a woman in Africa, I can understand a lot about mothering. And I can apply her image to reaching out to others with care and concern.

There are eight hundred languages spoken on the continent of Africa. How would you communicate in that environment? Economically, ecumenically, and in every other way the number of languages poses seemingly insurmountable challenges to forming relationships. No wonder there are tribal misunderstandings that lead to contention and violence. It is not uncommon to find reports in our newspapers each week of tragic deaths in a South African township or a central African republic.

Local leaders now encourage Church units in Africa to adopt one language per country. This seems an obvious solution, but it's still difficult. Older women depend on a tribal tongue. I feel for them because I know the frustration of trying to get something as simple as passport clearance when I cannot understand the language or voice inflections.

Lots of times we use the same words, but we don't mean the same thing. It has taken me a long time to figure out that when one of my relatives says, "That's fine," she may really mean, "I'm too tired to come up with a better solution," or "I really don't like it, but I won't object on this one," or "I don't care," or "I don't choose to deal with this issue right now."

The knack of communication goes far beyond words. If we only accepted the literal meaning of words, we might miss most of the true meaning. We have to learn to read body language and listen for innuendos.

I do better in a relationship where I don't feel I must walk on eggs. I am happiest when I can just say what's on my mind and hope the listener will understand my meaning even if my words are not as clear as I mean them to be.

Even a bridge built with good materials can fall if it is anchored in sand. So it is with communication—our bridges should be built on bedrock so our efforts will stand despite the storms that come. For young couples getting started in life—as we did, for example, building a medical practice and raising a family—life resembles a major hurricane. Sometimes in our early married years we felt good to have just survived the day. The trick of keeping equanimity, I've found, is to focus on what matters, to sink your foundations deep in strong values, and to enjoy what life offers.

I have learned relatively recently how hard it is to dig deep enough within to find and risk real feelings. The challenge for me is to open those real feelings to Joe, my spouse of forty-three years. I would suggest that one of the things that matters most is to make that spousal relationship number one, to build a bridge there that transcends every other link you create. If you and your spouse remain thoughtful, trusting, respectful, and communicative, most other things will fall into place.

To return to the image of bridges, remember they are built from shore to shore and must meet in the middle. "Building" is an active word. It implies effort. We must take initiative.

I suggest this exercise. Write down one thing that matters very much to you. When you have jotted this idea down, think, "How can I communicate that to my spouse? to my children? to my friends?" This mental exercise marks the beginning of action.

Goethe was right, of course. We should never let what matters least get in the way of what matters most. The trick is to know what matters most, then to plan how to live by that, how to make it known. The goal is to have our most important value etched clearly in our mind and heart, where it provides the tensile strength of our life's bridge.

# *Stability in These Times*

Our times have been termed the days of miracle and wonder. Supersonic airliners cross the ocean from Paris to New York in four hours. Implantation of artificial organs extends human life. Thanks to telecommunication satellites, telephone calls and faxed messages can encircle the globe almost instantly. Computing networks make possible storage and retrieval of vast networks of information. These are technological wonders.

Such innovations have made the impossible possible. At the same time, they have made our life more complex. We live at a tremendously accelerated pace of life. The power to extend human life has forced us to ask *when* life should be extended. And the constant bombardment of information requires that we process more and often conflicting data.

And the complexities multiply. Our world is not the same place today that it was last year or even yesterday.

The same is true within our individual lives. What a change a year or two – or even a few months – can make.

I am a very ordinary woman who has spent much of my life dealing with the day-to-day complications and joys of being a wife and a mother of four sons. Complications, like keeping enough milk in the refrigerator; joys, like having an even number of socks come out of the dryer. Complications, in managing a home with busy high school students and a bishop husband; joys, in seeing my sons prepared to serve missions, prepared for life. In the middle of the mothering phase of my life, I was not thinking about issues or forming philosophies. I was just dealing with one day at a time.

But there is life after sixty. The aging process may bring wrinkles and rigidity, but it also brings a time to contemplate. As I get older, I can see how the world has opened up because of many innovations, yet it's sometimes hard for me personally to make the changes necessary to take full advantage of them. In my own daily life I am constantly assaulted by much that is new.

I do my writing on a typewriter and pencil in my corrections. I have seen my secretary make the same changes in seconds on a computer. I can see how easy it is, but I still like a pencil. I am hardly used to the idea that a letter can be faxed over the telephone, and it is still embarrassing to be told by a car, "Your brake is on!"

We all have areas where we are resistant to change. I hear similar echoes in our society. The bywords of this time are coping, stress, future shock, megatrends, the lonely crowd. These bywords are daily reminders of our insecurity with the confrontations of change. Why do we resist change? What will give us the confidence necessary to accept change and incorporate that which is good? Stability.

As I define *stability,* it is not inflexibility or resistance to positive change. It does not mean exercising fewer choices or avoiding challenges. Stability is constancy of character or purpose, tenacity, steadfastness, reliability, and dependability. It is a grounding, a rooting, an anchor. Unfortunately, stability seems rarer as life goes faster.

One of the great joys of living in this age is the opportunity to create stability in our own lives. It can be a happy challenge. Five anchors have helped stabilize my life: testimony, relationships with others, charity, progress, and maturity.

My testimony developed early. I was blessed to grow up two doors away from my grandparents, who were guided throughout their life by impressions that I know came from simple, righteous living and complete faith. Their belief in the tenets of the gospel was so internalized that it was the foremost consideration in every circumstance, whether it was giving a healing blessing to an ill child, abandoning insurance selling to become custodian at the temple, or searching for the names of Scottish ancestors. Grandpa's "impressions" even prompted a move of a thousand miles to a new country, Canada. He wrote in his journal: "I prayed for guidance concerning my future. Then one spring morning in March of the following year, from a pamphlet which came in the mail, I read of a settlement in Raymond, Canada, and turning to my wife said, 'Mary Ann, I feel impressed to move to Raymond, Canada.' My wife felt as I did that the impression was from the right spirit."

This is my heritage, a firm foundation. Like my grandparents, I believe in a God who strengthens me, helps me, and causes me to stand by his righteous, omnipotent hand. This belief is the basis of my life.

Stability is the fruit of internalizing the gospel, of listening, praying, searching, lifting up our voices to attain wisdom from the Lord. In Proverbs 2:2–5, we read: "Incline thine ear unto wisdom, and apply thine heart to understanding; yea, if thou criest after knowledge, and liftest up thy voice for understanding; if thou seekest her as silver, and searchest for her as for hid treasures; then shalt thou understand the fear of the Lord, and find the knowledge of God."

Even though I have a heritage of gospel belief, I have made the choice to develop a testimony. I accept the responsibilities that go with my choice to follow the living prophet, to embrace currently revealed and emphasized truth.

Testimony is a result of choice, not of circumstances. This world is full of soul-troubling injustices: homeless children, innocent victims of war or ignorance, people alone and unloved. The wonderful thing about life is that despite the injustices of this world, each of us still has the choice to believe.

Some people equate stability with ease. The two are not the same. A friend pointed out that while we sympathize with trying and testing situations, positive circumstances can be difficult also. She said, "Women who have stable, happy lives are made to feel almost scorned." She had been at lunch with friends—one who was having serious problems with a son, and another whose husband's business was failing—and they said to her, "What do you know of trouble? I wish all I had to worry about were Christmas stockings for my grandchildren." My friend said she felt almost guilty to admit in this group that her children were successful and happily married, and that her grandchildren were healthy. Perhaps trials or the lack of them have been individualized for our own personal growth, "customized challenges," in the words of Elder Neal A. Maxwell.

We hear often that the Lord gives trials to those he loves, that those who have trials are thereby proven worthy. I believe that the Lord does love us as individuals, whether or not we have great trials. In good circumstances or bad, we can make choices that will build our testimonies.

We must seek a testimony. Actively seeking involves more than just looking. The prophet Jacob tells us, "Remember that ye are free to act for yourselves." (2 Nephi 10:23.) At some point in life, we must each make a decision,

"I will do *this* with my life." Then we do not let circumstances determine our actions or drive us away from the truth. In all seasons of life, testimony is a conscious choice that gives meaning to everything else.

My second anchor is my relationships with others. Friends are valuable to me. One of my favorite ways to spend an evening is to invite six diverse, but compatible, friends to my home for dinner and a lively visit. Cultivating a variety of friends, including those in my immediate and extended family, has brought me stability. I love the stimulation of developing friendships with many types of people, and I value what they teach me.

Friends multiply my store of knowledge in the most pleasant ways. I can hardly wait to see an attorney friend when I have read about a legal issue and have questions. I solved many of the world's problems with my friend Donna when we walked together in the mornings. My son, a biochemist, sent me a book titled *DNA for Beginners* so we could converse intelligently about his work. Three of my friends who are outstanding scriptorians open up my mind and pour in their understanding. There is so much I want to learn, and with friends I am free to ask questions and to be nurtured in an encouraging way. I can provide the setting for this in my home or in the park or in a car on the way to a symphony performance. It doesn't take an expensive menu or a lavish centerpiece. I have had some wonderful conversations over curdly soup and rolls that have burned on the bottom and are doughy in the middle. I have had a fascinating discussion about a trip to the bird refuge with my grandson over a peanut butter and jelly sandwich. I could not live in isolation. I respond to family and friends. They encourage me, they buoy me up, they make me feel worthwhile. Friends are gifts from the Lord that bring stability to my life.

Friendships are enhanced through exercising charity—another of my anchors. All life is enriched through charity. The high status of charity is extolled by Paul in the thirteenth chapter of First Corinthians. No quality is as enduring or comforting as charity. Charity *never* faileth. Charity is a constant, dependable, reliable, stable force.

I have learned over the years that charitable people have all the real fun. They are the people others are drawn to. They expend their energies in positive ways that bring light and energy to others and themselves. This could be an actual description of my friend Carolyn, who works in the Young Women office. I have seen her give a treasured shell to encourage an unhappy employee. I watched her rejoice with a handicapped former student who proudly reported getting A's and B's at the community college. I am aware of her deep concern and constant caring for aged parents — even though it is by long distance. Nearly every Church employee knows Carolyn, and I suspect they make many more trips to her office than necessary, to bask in the light she radiates.

It is a marvel to me that charity can be exercised in the smallest ways. We find stability as we take small opportunities to serve and get support from others. I was comforted by a hand-delivered note from my Relief Society president when she knew I was nervous over an important assignment. On the other hand, I felt the joy of serving when I tended a newborn baby so her parents could attend a sunrise Easter service. As we serve, we tacitly send the message: "You are okay and I am here." I remember feeling the overwhelming goodness and support of others when our first son went on his mission. He received encouragement from such unexpected sources that it intensified my awareness of the love that was shown.

Charity is the context for all we do, for it is our major means of becoming Christlike. If charity is the pure love of Christ, then learning its laws is the way to know more about our Savior. No pursuit will bring more stability to our lives than this.

I can feel good about myself if I can detect that in some way I am a better person today than I was a year ago. This is my fourth anchor. An awareness of progression, even if it is small in the eyes of the world, provides a stabilizing sense of worth. The challenging part is to separate real progess from that which only appears to be moving forward.

By whose criteria do we measure? The Church's? Society's? Progression is so individual that each person must set an individual plan. For example, if the criteria for progress were having a good husband and a large family, some women would feel they had lost out. If our criteria were academic, a mother of many small children might feel that she was not progressing because she was not continuing with a formal education. An older woman could feel useless because she lacked a career opportunity; a couple, if they were not serving on a mission. Happily, progression is measured in many more subtle ways than counting numbers of children or degrees.

Several years ago we read about Molly Mormon and Patty Perfect and laughed—maybe a little painfully—because we all understood the stereotype. In these extremes we saw how easily we create barriers that stymie our individuality and our true progression.

Do you remember Aesop's fable of the lazy grasshopper and the prudent ants? During the summer the ants are busy gathering a store of food for the winter while the grasshopper, despite the ants' warning of a long, cold winter ahead, sings, dances, and plays his fiddle. At the BYU Women's Conference in 1987, Louise Plummer gave some thoughts on "being a grasshopper" based on this fable. She said, "I always wondered if there was room in a family of ants . . . or room in a church of ants for a grasshopper. . . . [I] fear that ants will not accept me unless I am just like them." (*A Heritage of Faith,* ed. Mary E. Stovall and Carol Cornwall Madsen [Salt Lake City: Deseret Book, 1988], p. 189.) She concludes that both grasshoppers, whose work may be bringing happiness to others, and ants who store the food are necessary. We just need to remember that "grasshoppers work differently from ants." Nourishing the body is necessary, but the soul needs to be fed too. Our methods of feeding either may vary.

Based on someone else's standards, we might all be losers. When we measure ourselves against arbitrary standards, we tend not to progress because we are focused on the wrong kinds of things. In such circumstances we might be compared to those Jews described in the Book of Mormon whose blindness came from "looking beyond the mark." (Jacob 4:14.) Stability comes in my life when I focus on the things that are mine to do.

We discover what our own life tasks are by asking the right questions. Perhaps the most important question we can ask is, "What is the Lord's will for me?" That is our gauge for progression.

Ponder the questions prophets have asked, as noted in the scriptures: "How is it possible that ye can lay hold upon every good thing?" (Moroni 7:20.) "What think ye of Christ?" (Matthew 22:42.) "What manner of men [or women] ought ye to be?" (3 Nephi 27:27.)

And then relish the answers: "By faith . . . lay [ye] hold upon every good thing." What think ye of Christ? "He is the Lord." What manner of men ought ye to be? "Even as I am."

The answers I have found as I've asked about my own mission and path of progression have brought boundless stability to my life. They have given me a sense of purpose and vision, a sustaining nourishment of body and soul.

Progress is an individual matter. Our achievement should be measured against our own past accomplishments. Progression brings stability through the satisfaction of accomplishing goals. There is much more happiness in becoming something than in getting something.

My fifth anchor is maturity. I found it delightfully refreshing to hear Barbara Bush, wife of the president of the United States, say on nationwide television at her husband's inauguration, "See this styled hair? See this designer suit? Take a good look because you probably won't see them again." Women loved it because she was saying, "There is no artificial standard. I am comfortable with myself as I am, and I want you to know it." That's maturity—the ability to happily face yourself. Maturity is what allows us to accept ourselves even when we are not all we would want to be.

We should never abandon the quest for a better self. But neither should we allow ourselves to become immobilized, thinking we are nobody. One of Satan's greatest tools is to convince us that we are worth nothing, to lead us to deny our divine heritage. He would have us "be miserable like unto himself." (2 Nephi 2:27.) It is stabilizing to be able to say, "This is who I am, and I am happy to live with me."

Such maturity allows us to accept who and where we are. This same maturity can give us the moral courage to make our actions consistent with our knowlege of right and wrong, that is, to be "doers of the word." I think a "doer of the word" is that person who has become integrated—sufficiently mature—to act on her beliefs, especially when they don't conform to the popular views of the day. James says it this way: "Be ye doers of the word, and not hearers only, deceiving your own selves. For if any be a hearer of the word, and not a doer, he is like unto a man beholding his natural face in a glass: For he beholdeth himself, and goeth his way, and straightway forgetteth what manner of man he was." (James 1:22–24.)

Mature people, regardless of age, are able to face themselves and act in positive ways despite flaws they may see. We all have parts of our character we don't like. Mature people "press forward with a steadfastness in Christ, having a perfect brightness of hope, and a love of God and all men." (2 Nephi 31:20.)

Another scripture that is meaningful to me comes from First Corinthians. It is compelling to me that at the end of Paul's marvelous discussion of charity is a statement about maturity: "When I was a child, I spake as a child, I understood as a child, I thought as a child: but when I became a man, I put away childish things." (1 Corinthians 13:11.) As we put away childish things, as we mature spiritually, we understand what we see, we know who we are, and we act upon what we believe.

Stability is possible in our lives. Through testimony, friendship, charity, progression, and maturity we can maintain lasting stability, which will endure despite the clatter of these changing times.

# Heroes and Heroines

I must admit that I think every woman I have ever met is great. Strength and capability and talent abound in every woman, not just in those who've been written about in history textbooks. The women I admire show resilience in the face of problems; they overcome great odds; they demonstrate resourcefulness, courage, the pioneer spirit, and other magnificent qualities.

We've all had women in our past who have touched our lives deeply — perhaps a mother, sister, aunt, schoolteacher, church member, or a friend so close that we are what Anne of Green Gables called "kindred spirits." It's usually someone we admire, someone who has given something to our spirits, someone we love deeply. These special women in our lives touch people, they lift, they help us see our worth. They are the "givers" of the world.

Certain women like this have had their stories documented because what they've done is remarkable or praiseworthy. Esther of the Bible is a good example. When she decided to try to save her people from Haman's plot to kill all the Jews, she showed great courage and faith. For added strength, she asked the Jews and her "maidens" to fast for her for three days. Her commitment to her people was so great that she said, "So will I go in unto the king, which is not according to the law: and if I perish, I perish." (Esther 4:16.)

Another woman of great courage was a thirteen-year-old pioneer named Mary Goble. Her family was converted in Sussex, England, and she left with her parents and five brothers and sisters to travel to Utah. Despite a hard ocean crossing, with seasickness, a mutiny on board, and thick fog for several days, the family landed safely in Boston. They then took the train to Iowa City, where they purchased two yoke of oxen, one yoke of cows, a wagon and a tent. In Iowa Mary's small sister, not quite two, who was suffering from measles, got wet in a fierce thunderstorm and died. They had to bury her there.

Mary wrote:

> We traveled [on] ... till we got to the Platte River. That was the last walk I ever had with our mother. We caught up with the handcart companies that day. We watched them cross the river. There were great lumps of ice floating down the river. It was bitter cold. The next morning there were fourteen dead in camp through the cold. We went back to camp and went to prayers. They sang, "Come, Come Ye Saints, No Toil Nor Labor Fear." I wondered what made my mother cry.
>
> That night my mother took sick and the next morning my little sister was born. ... She lived six weeks and died for the want of nourishment.

Not long after, Mary went to get some fresh water from a spring for her mother, but got lost in the deep snow. Her legs and feet were frozen by the time the rescuers got to her. They rubbed her legs with snow to revive the circulation, but her feet were badly frostbitten and could not be restored. The weather continued to be cruel. A few days later her sister May was frozen to death. Her brother James died three days later. Her mother died the day they arrived in Salt Lake City.

A kind bishop took the remaining family members to a house in his ward and fed them. Early the next morning Brigham Young and a doctor came to see them. Mary wrote, "When [Brigham] saw our condition, our feet frozen and our mother dead, tears rolled down his cheeks. The doctor wanted to cut my feet off at the ankle, but President Young said no, just cut off the toes and I promise you, you will never have to take them off any further."

But instead of Mary's feet getting better, they got worse. The doctor advised her to have them amputated, but she said no, and told him what Brigham Young had promised. The doctor told her there was no chance her feet could be saved. But she had faith.

> One day I sat there crying, my feet were hurting me so, when a little old woman knocked at the door. She said she had felt that someone needed her there, and asked me what was the matter. I showed her my feet and told her the promise Brother Brigham Young had given me. She said, "Yes, and with the help of the Lord we will save them yet." She made a poultice and put it on my feet...every day. At the end of three months my feet were well. ("Life of Mary Ann Goble Pay," as quoted in *Improvement Era*, June 1970, pp. 40–41.)

I am uplifted by Mary's courage, but I also appreciate the fact that a loving sister behind the scenes was inspired to help a young woman she didn't even know. She exemplified the words of Emily Woodmansee: "The errand of angels is given to women, and this is a gift that as sisters we claim: To do whatsoever is gentle and human, To cheer and to bless in humanity's name." ("As Sisters in Zion," Hymns, no. 309.) We have much to salute in the women of the past. There is a great nobility in women.

There are other remarkable women whose names we do not even know who possess heroic characteristics. Take, for example, Nephi's wife. We know she was one of the daughters of Ishmael. When she and Nephi were married, the families of Lehi and Ishmael were living in the wilderness in a tent. (1 Nephi 16:6–7.) (From my backpacking days I know what that is like!) She bore her children in the wilderness. She traveled to a new land where she built a home and raised a family. I know that feeling, too. When I was first married I moved with my husband to New York City. To a woman who had grown up in a small town of two thousand souls, New York was a strange new land.

Nephi's wife belonged to an extended family whose relationships were very stressful. When her brothers-in-law tried to kill her husband and were continually disagreeing with him and contesting his counsel, she strongly supported Nephi. On shipboard on the way to the new land, after Laman and Lemuel bound Nephi, he said, "and also my wife with her tears and prayers . . . did not soften the hearts of my brethren that they would loose me." (1 Nephi 18:19.) How that woman must have grieved when she saw her husband abused and her mother-in-law sick! I think Nephi's wife was a great woman. She must have been, to endure the life that was hers to live and to be so supportive of her husband.

Some other heroic women in the Book of Mormon were the mothers of the 2,000 stripling warriors who fought with Helaman. Scripture tells us that these sons "did obey and observe to perform every word of command with exactness; yea, and even according to their faith it was done unto them; and I did remember the words which they said unto me that their mothers had taught them." (Alma 57:21.) We don't know the name of any one of those mothers, and yet the story of their sons' courage and faith is a direct reflection of the teachings of these good women—heroines every one. Our own mothers may rank with these women as heroines in our lives.

I'd also include as a heroine Abish, the Lamanite woman who was a servant to Lamoni's queen when Ammon gave his powerful testimony and the household of King Lamoni was converted. Remember that King Lamoni lay as if dead. The queen sent for Ammon, who told her the king was not dead, and she believed him. I love his response to the queen, "Blessed art thou because of thy exceeding faith; I say unto thee, woman, there has not been such great faith among all the people of the Nephites." The king did arise, as Alma had said, and the testimony he bore was so powerful that he and the queen, and even Ammon "sunk . . . with joy . . . being overpowered by the Spirit." And Abish, the servant, was the only one left standing. The scriptures tell us that she had "been converted unto the Lord for many years, on account of a remarkable vision of her father." I think Abish recognized her opportunity—that "by making known unto the people what had happened . . . , it would cause them to believe in the power of God, therefore she ran forth from house to house, making it known unto the people" that the household of King Lamoni had found the true faith. (Alma 19:10–17.) I think her name should have been Sister Abish, an early missionary.

Abish reminds me of Yen, a Chinese friend who lived much of her life in South Africa. When she returned to Taiwan she married and she and her husband were converted to the Church. That was more than seventeen years ago. Since that time she has divorced and is supporting her teenage daughter and living in southern California. Yen has been a stalwart in defending the teachings of the gospel. She has clung tenaciously to her faith when it has not been popular with her family. They derided her for the devotion, time, and money she expended for the Church, while they were financially very successful. But she quietly practiced her religion. After all those years Yen told me recently, "Elaine, my sisters have come to respect me." I class her as a heroine.

I like to remember the obscure heroes and heroines because they do important things without having to travel the world or make a lot of money or be famous. The people that I most look up to are those you would probably never hear of any other place, like my mother, Lovina, and my grandfather John, my neighbor Pete next door, and Sharon, the ward Relief Society president. They are names you wouldn't know, but their actions you would acknowledge and admire just as I do.

I like to include the wives of the General Authorities as unsung heroines of our generation because of the strength they add and their behind-the-scenes support of their husbands doing an important work. In my case, it is the other way around. I couldn't do my job without the support of my husband. He doesn't do dinners, but he does everything else. General Authority wives willingly sacrifice family life with their husbands and keep their families together, generally by themselves. They are often sensitive to feelings and happenings that their husbands might miss. I was particularly aware of this when Sister Barbara Perry brought the wives of seven military leaders to our building so we could tell them a little about the auxiliaries of the Church. Sister Perry was entertaining these wives while Elder L. Tom Perry was holding some strategic meetings with their husbands. The outcome of those meetings would be influenced to quite an extent by the impressions of those seven women, only one of whom was a Latter-day Saint.

If we and our family members wish to profit from having heroes and heroines and role models to emulate, we have only to open our eyes to those around us. Reflect on your own life experiences. Was there a favorite teacher, or maybe a person in your neighborhood, who made life better for you when you were a child? Is there someone you have worked with who has made a difference? Whom do you look up to in your family?

I often speak admiringly of my sister Jean. I am always flattered when somebody tells me that I look like her. Because of my love and respect for her, I want to have her approval. Those closest to us are the ones we tend to admire because they're the ones we know the best. I realize that the better I know people, the better I like them and the more I admire them.

Since we're most likely to model ourselves after the people we know the best, we ought to get to know the best people. We should choose friends who love the Lord and read the scriptures and go to church and live the laws of God. Then we need to be the kind of people that others will seek out because we do those things ourselves.

Think about the times when you yourself have been an unsung hero. Maybe you were in the shadows, doing the work for which someone else took credit, or holding the curtain while someone else took the bows. My office staff fits into this category. You don't know their names, and you don't know their contributions, but I do. I have several unsung heroines who knock themselves out on my behalf, but it is my picture that gets into the paper.

Was there ever a time when you fell back so someone else didn't have to be last? Perhaps it was in a family race or a competitive game. I know my grandpa lost a lot of games of checkers so I could win and gain confidence. Maybe you chose to be last—to bring up the rear—so you could be sure that no one got lost along the way.

In this world where media productions bring new faces and names into the headlines every month, it is hard to isolate what is real and lasting. To my way of thinking, fame is fleeting, but heroism is something that endures. Heroism is based upon truth, that is, upon the principles of the gospel of Jesus Christ, which encompasses all truth. Fame is Madonna; heroism is Helen Keller. Fame is Oprah Winfrey; heroism is Mother Teresa. Fame is Joe Montana; heroism is Spencer W. Kimball. Heroism is basing your life upon things that last.

To live heroically is to understand that there is a difference between making a difference in the world and making a splash. I want the women of the Church to make a difference. I want you to make a difference because you can and because, without you, the world would be a darker place.

We do not lack for heroes or heroines today. They are all around us if we look for them. They are you.

# "Distinguished for Their Zeal"

he relationship among Relief Society sisters means a lot to me. I like the words from Jacob 1:19: "And we did magnify our office unto the Lord, taking upon us the responsibility, answering the sins of the people upon our own heads if we did not teach them the word of God with all diligence; wherefore, by laboring with our might their blood might not come upon our garments; otherwise their blood would come upon our garments, and we would not be found spotless at the last day."

Can you imagine what it would be like in Relief Society if each sister took full responsibility for her neighbors, her friends, those she visit teaches? The world would be different. I would like to see each Latter-day Saint, without being asked, take responsibility for the well-being of every other individual.

One of the points of emphasis in the mission statement of Relief Society is to "Bless the Individual Woman," whether she is nineteen or ninety, single, married, tall, short, with red hair or black hair, brown or blonde.

My friend and counselor in the general Relief Society presidency, Chieko Okazaki, shared an interesting concept about perspective. When you sit on a mountain top and look at a valley of trees below, all you see is an ocean of green beneath you. No one thing stands out. But if you come down from the mountain and walk into the valley, you can see that each tree and bush is different. Some are short, some tall, some have broad leaves, some have unusual bark. Each is distinctive.

As I look into a sea of faces, I can't determine exclusive differences in people, but I know that each is an individual. I think about the value of distinctiveness, about the value of personal spiritual and mental preparation, and about each one taking responsibility for magnifying her office.

A wonderful verse in the book of Alma describes the people of Anti-Nephi-Lehi, those Lamanites who were converted to the Church and moved to the land of Jershon: "And they were . . . numbered among the people who were of the church of God. And they were also distinguished for their zeal towards God, and also towards men; for they were perfectly honest and upright in all things; and they were firm in the faith of Christ, even unto the end." (Alma 27:27.) I'd like to adapt these words to describe us, the people who make up the church of God in these days.

What does it mean to be "distinguished for their zeal"? The dictionary says that having "zeal" means to pursue with passionate ardor, to be ardent, to have earnest intent.

There's a difference between having zeal and being a zealot. Traditionally, a "zealot" has been someone who was extreme in his or her beliefs and actions. To be "zealous," on the other hand, is to be ardent and eager in our work. It connotes a sense of balance and understanding of how what we do and say and think fits into the broader context of what is going on in the world. To be zealous is to be Ezra Taft Benson. To be a zealot is to be Saddam Hussein, out of touch and out of control.

One way to illustrate this concept is to compare two leaders from the

Book of Mormon: Captain Moroni and Amalickiah. Amalickiah is described as "a man of cunning device and a man of many flattering words, that he led away the hearts of many people to do wickedly; yea, and to seek to destroy the church of God, and to destroy the foundation of liberty which God had granted unto them, or which blessing God had sent upon the face of the land for the righteous' sake." (Alma 46:10.)

Moroni, on the other hand, wrote upon the title of liberty, "In memory of our God, our religion, and freedom, and our peace, our wives, and our children." The scriptures say that when he had fastened on his own armor, he took the title of liberty upon its pole and "bowed himself to the earth, and he prayed mightily unto his God for the blessings of liberty to rest upon his brethren, so long as there should a band of Christians remain to possess the land." (Alma 46:12–13.)

What a difference between these two men! Amalickiah, the zealot, sought for his personal gain at any cost. Moroni, the zealous, sought for the good of his brethren and for the cause of righteousness.

We need to be zealous in the same causes that motivated Captain Moroni. The things he wrote on the title of liberty are the best things in life for which to be zealous: our belief in God, which is the bedrock of all things we do; our religion; the freedom that allows us to exercise our religious rights; and our peace and families. These are the great causes—causes that are worthy of our laying our lives on the line.

What is it that distinguishes us? When we say that people are distinguished we generally mean that they bear themselves well, they dress well, they handle themselves well. What does it mean to be distinguished *for* something? We talk about distinguished artists, distinguished composers. How about being known as the distinguished Christian, a woman distinguished for her charitable service? How can we be distinguished for our zeal?

Barbara Winder, our former general Relief Society president, immediately comes to my mind. She is a compassionate soul, tender and caring and willing to work. She was released from her calling as president to go help her husband direct the mission in Czechoslovakia, from a two-room apartment, standing in lines to get such common foods as cauliflower and potatoes.

As we examine the areas of our lives where we exercise zeal, do we find that we are most zealous in professional pursuits? Or zealous about perfect make-up? About earning money or shopping? Are young women more zealous about getting a degree or getting a date? How about as a daughter or a mother or a Sunday School teacher? In what areas are we distinguished for our zeal?

Just like the people of Ammon, we need to choose what we will be distinguished for. And if we choose as they did to be "perfectly honest and upright in all things" and "firm in the faith of Christ, even unto the end," we will be zealous in all the best causes.

Sometimes we misinterpret zealousness as busyness. Like the great distinction between being zealous and being a zealot, being engaged in many causes does not necessarily mean we are engaged in the best causes.

Let us be clear about what it is that deserves and demands our zeal and not dissipate our energies — spiritual, mental, emotional, and physical — in any old cause, but rather in the best cause. There are many good things vying for our attention, but the good and the better need to be subjugated to the best. I like the saying, "It is not enough to be busy. What are we busy about?"

I believe that in order for us to be distinguished for our zeal as Christians, as members of The Church of Jesus Christ of Latter-day Saints, we must be clear, we must be focused, we must place our energies into the best things.

*119*

If you have served a mission and have gone through the Missionary Training Center, you likely know Mary Ellen Edmunds. Mary Ellen is single and serves on our Relief Society board. At age twenty-two, she served her first mission. Her focus in life ever since has been great and enduring missionary work and humanitarian service. She has served in Thailand, the Philippines, Taiwan, Africa. This has been her lifetime cause. It is reflected in her countenance and in her interaction with people. When I greet her, "How are you, Mary Ellen?" she inevitably responds, "Happy." It seems to me that the people whom I would define as being distinguished for their zeal are living out their commitment to their covenants and to the gospel of Jesus Christ. They are both leaders and followers.

Let us be distinguished for our zeal. Let us be known as women who have chosen the best.

# Tools for Touching Lives

# The Mission of Relief Society

We are on the threshold of a new decade and new things are happening. In the years since 1980, dramatic advances have taken place in the Church: new temples have been built, our meetings have been consolidated into a three-hour block, many missions have been opened.

For the decade ahead we have refocused the mission of Relief Society. The organization and the goals are the same, but we have expanded our focus in order to address the changing needs in today's world. We have to consider worldwide implications.

I want to share with you what we consider to be the mission of Relief Society for this new decade and how it is going to meet the needs of our sisters. As you read the following points that make up our mission statement, I would encourage you particularly to think how it blesses an individual and how each part of it encourages individual action.

## Build Personal Testimony

The first point of our mission statement is to Build Personal Testimony. That is the foundation for everything else we do. I have grown to realize what a difference my personal testimony makes in my life.

Since my call as general Relief Society president, many people have asked about my younger life: what I did that prepared me for this job, and what influential people made a difference in my life. I have welcomed those questions because they have helped me recognize more than ever the events in my life that have led me to my personal testimony.

I was raised in a small Latter-day Saint community in Cardston, Canada. The temple was just a half block away from my house, so you can imagine its influence in our neighborhood. Everybody shared the same values. Everybody participated in the social events. We were all friends. I thought this was a way of life for the whole world. My testimony was formed even before I was aware of it.

But I do remember the exact moment when I became aware that I had a testimony and how much difference it made in my life. It wasn't until my husband and I had moved to New York. I remember thinking, "You do believe in the gospel of Jesus Christ. You believe what you are hearing or you wouldn't make all the effort to go to church." It was an instant of realization that made all the difference to me. My testimony didn't stop growing then, and I didn't stop realizing and appreciating it.

I try to walk every morning with my good friend. I think I notice with greater appreciation than ever the beautiful world that Heavenly Father has provided for us. That is part of my testimony. The flowers seem more perfect every year; the children are more precious; the music is more thrilling; the grass is greener; the mountains are more beautiful. I feel that every time I acknowledge these wonders, every time I notice them, it is a way for my testimony to grow. We have to be aware of what is around us, aware of the Lord's blessings.

In Thornton Wilder's play "Our Town," the character Emily was allowed to come back to earth for one day after her death. As she prepared to return to the cemetery, she looked around at her beloved Grover's Corners and said good-bye to everything. Then she asked the stage manager, "Do any human beings ever realize life while they live it—every, every minute?"

There is no reason why we can't realize and value the wonder of life. Sometimes we simply don't notice. We have to desire a testimony and look for it in everything that we see.

Another way to build personal testimony is by reading the scriptures. It is an inspiring way to know what the Lord would have us do right now. We pray, we ponder, and we go to the temple. Beyond that, we share our testimonies, and that is a wonderful way to help them grow. This doesn't mean that we have to stand in testimony meeting, or that we say exactly some prescribed words. Sometimes sharing a testimony is as simple as saying, "I really believe that." But this can only happen as we have interaction with other people. It is important for us to be together and seriously talk—talk about things that are in our hearts that really matter. It is a way to develop testimony.

In addition to studying the scriptures, pondering concepts from books is a great way to build testimony. I can't think every original or grand thought in this world, but I am grateful for others who do. When I read such inspiring thoughts, they add something to my life and give me the opportunity to seek and to increase my testimony.

"Actively seeking" implies much more than just looking for a testimony. Building personal testimony has to be a high priority in our lives. Then, when we experience an event or some instance or moment of truth, the Spirit bears witness to us. As Jacob said, "The Spirit speaketh the truth and lieth not." (Jacob 4:13.) The Lord said also, "By my Spirit will I enlighten them." (D&C 76:10.)

We can share, we can motivate, we can talk to each other, but the Spirit is what builds testimony.

It is through everyday experiences of appreciating the world, of talking to our friends and loving them, and of giving service that we build testimony. We seek and we notice our blessings. In everything we do in Relief Society we make personal testimony paramount.

## Bless the Individual Woman

The second point of our mission statement is to Bless the Individual Woman. Do you remember the story in Third Nephi when the Savior visited the people on the American continent after his crucifixion? As recorded in chapter 11, he introduced himself and then said some very important things: "Behold, I am Jesus Christ, whom the prophets testified shall come into the world. And behold, I am the light and the life of the world; and I have drunk out of that bitter cup which the Father hath given me, and have glorified the Father in taking upon me the sins of the world." First he announced himself, and he could be easily seen. You would think the multitude would believe he was indeed the Christ. But then he said this, "Arise and come forth unto me, that ye may thrust your hands into my side, and also that ye may feel the prints of the nails in my hands and in my feet, that ye may know that I am the God of Israel, and the God of the whole earth, and have been slain for the sins of the world."

Then this significant event took place: "And it came to pass that the multitude went forth, and thrust their hands into his side, and did feel the prints of the nails in his hands and in his feet; and this they did do, going forth one by one until they had all gone forth." (3 Nephi 11:10–11, 14–15.) That was a big crowd—a multitude. They all felt his hands and feet, one by one. This experience wasn't just for some. It wasn't just for those who didn't have children, or for those who didn't have other occupations. One by one, every one of them went up. The Lord is concerned about every individual. That is what he tells us in the scriptures. In Relief Society, we too desire to bless each individual woman.

Wonderful letters come to our office from women throughout the world, including this one from a happy mother in Denver:

> I love being a mother. I love reading with my children and teaching them the gospel. . . . They are two of my best friends.
>
> I am grateful for the creativity and imaginations of my children. They have been playing with a large cardboard box for several months now. It is a time machine, a space ship, a computer, an airplane, and a hover craft. I am grateful for their ability to enjoy such things. Of course, they also love to watch a video, go to a friend's house where they can play Nintendo and play computer games. That's okay. At least they understand the culture or a bit of it of the day. But it is not their mainstay. On the other hand, a Nintendo game is a lot easier to keep clean than two laundry baskets filled with dress-up clothes and stuff. We don't have a computer, but I am sure it is easier to keep track of than paints, markers, crayons, paper, etc. I have to keep reminding myself that I am caring for two wonderful spirits entrusted to me by the Lord and in thirteen short years, Hanna will be eighteen and there won't be anyone to spill the dress-up baskets all over the floor. I am very grateful to Heavenly Father for sharing that insight with me.

Now let me cite another letter from a Relief Society president in a singles' ward. She writes of her concerns for her sisters and how she wants to bless them:

> In the past several weeks, my concern and that of the other leaders of the ward has heightened as the most stalwart of my worthy sisters, not numbering a few, have reached a point of resignation in their discouragement. These are temple workers, Sunday School teachers, Relief Society teachers, faithful visiting teachers, and intelligent, attractive women, varying in age, many over the age of thirty. It is frightening and saddening to me. I desire to serve these women effectively. Perhaps as women there is more we can do to be an influence for good things, that our ward may be united in purpose, love, and kindness one to another; that collectively we may learn to foster correct choices; to know our Father's will and do it.

Isn't that a plea? I know she is going to succeed with that attitude, for she feels deeply her responsibility.

I include a letter from Massachusetts. This sister said:

> Ever since I joined this wonderful Church five years ago, I felt that Relief Society was definitely not for me. You see, my life has always been oriented towards raising my sons. I have spent most of my fascinating womanhood practicing soccer or wrestling or exploring mucky caves or building bonfires for cookouts or helping to design better paper airplanes. I really have had a hard time identifying with Relief Society. I really do bake bread but my eight-year-old son loves to knead it and we end up with flour everywhere. When we have fish for dinner, it means that Mom helps dig the worms

and show the boys how to hook them on the line. The fish we eat are often very tiny and sometimes a few scales end up on our plate. None of this is covered in the Relief Society manual.

What stands out in my mind about those three letters is that each writer has a common theme. Each of them is serving as she is able, according to the needs around her.

We associate certain words with our aim to Bless the Individual Woman. One is diversity. Think about the Relief Society sisters whom you know. Are any two of them alike? They are not. I am concerned about valuing diversity because we have an increasing diversity of women in our Church. We need to give our attention to the individual woman, to think inclusively, instead of exclusively. We need to think in terms of "the one," not just of singles or young mothers or the elderly as groups.

The transitions of life are important to remember too. Women in transition need special attention. Young Adults moving into Relief Society from the Young Women's program may need a particular welcome and assurances that they belong. Divorce is a common kind of transition. Sometimes the newly married have a hard time adjusting, as do the newly widowed or mothers with new babies. All are in stages of transition.

I am in a state of transition in my neighborhood. It really hit me hard one Saturday when my friend Amy died. Amy had been the mainstay of our neighborhood, and her passing was easier to accept because she had been terribly sick and she was eighty-five years old and she had lived a fruitful, wonderful life. But the neighborhood somehow is not going to be the same without Amy. So, even though I accepted her death in my head, I thought, "I need to go for a walk. I haven't had any exercise. I'll call JoAnn, she'll go with me." I called JoAnn and she said, "I really haven't been feeling very well today, Elaine. I don't feel like walking." I thought, "That's all right; I'll go get Dorothy." I went by Dorothy's house, but I could see that she had company. My long-time walking partner, Donna, had recently moved away. So I went walking by myself, having discovered that this time of transition was harder than I had imagined it would be. We all need a little extra help at such times.

### Develop and Exercise Charity

Consider the motto of Relief Society: "Charity Never Faileth." It thrills me to hear women around the world say those words, because I know they believe them. They are powerful words. "Charity Never Faileth." Charity is not something we do now and again. It's a way of thinking, a way of living. It is an attitude that we adopt.

My counselor Chieko Okazaki taught me something about this. She said, "We have to be 'kigatsuku.'" I said, "Chieko, I can't even say it. What is it?" "Kigatsuku," she said. "You know. When I was a young girl my mother taught me to be a 'kigatsuku' girl." When Chieko's mother was doing the dishes she would say, "Now, if you were a 'kigatsuku' girl, what would you do?" Chieko would think, "I would get the dish towel and wipe the dishes." "Kigatsuku" means looking around for things to do and then going ahead and doing them without being told. That is what it means to have an attitude of charity.

How do you give service in your neighborhood? People in your area need whatever you have to give. We have to look for needs and then make ourselves available to fill them.

The whole Relief Society program is a wonderful tool for serving individuals. Homemaking meetings and Sunday classes, visiting teachers and individuals, all can be vehicles for charity. When we give service it unites us together as sisters, teaches skills, and builds self-esteem. Service accomplishes the purposes of Relief Society.

One wonderful example of using a Relief Society meeting as an opportunity for service was when sisters of a stake in Draper, Utah, decided they would make quilts for the women in prison. In one day they put up and finished seventy-five quilts, which they later took to the women at the prison. Think of the implications of that. Think of what happened when women came together to do something for someone else. Think of what happened to those who received this lovely gift: they learned that someone was thinking about them, when they could easily feel forgotten. Wonderful things can happen when service is given and received.

When I think about charity, I think also about my own visiting teachers. Shortly after I was called to this position, one of them, Judy, came to see me at ten o'clock at night. She said, "Elaine, I haven't been able to get you before now, but I wish I could share with you the feeling that came over me when I heard your name called in conference. I just sat there stunned and this feeling came over me that said, 'I've got to take care of that woman.' " How I appreciated that! How important visiting teaching is to the whole concept of exercising charity.

Charity is right in the middle of our mission statement. We put it there intentionally, because we think charity in Relief Society acts as the keystone does in an arch. Charity is what holds everything else in the program together.

## *Strengthen Families*

Our fourth point is to Strengthen Families. The variety of families in the Church is staggering. Think of the kinds: traditional families, single-mother or single-father families, combined families, part-member families, less-active families, families with or without children. All families need strengthening.

One woman wrote to me:

> I am a single mother with two small boys, and I've been divorced for two years. In that amount of time I've found out how cruel it can be to be alone. I have no family.... I pay a full tithe, attend the temple regularly, my boy has been ordained a deacon, we've done baptisms for the dead together, my younger boy is in Scouts, I teach Sunday School, read the *Ensign* from the front to back cover, read the scriptures, clean my house, mow the lawn, weed the garden and sit alone, night after night. People in my ward know I'm single; yet my bishop has never visited my home, nor have the elders. I'm alone on Christmas and Thanksgiving. Yet I cook goodies and give them away. We are never invited to go anywhere or do anything, and we feel we've been cast aside.

Doesn't that hurt your heart? Do you know a family like that? What could you do to help strengthen such a family?

We want also to strengthen and support mothers who have chosen to stay at home with their children. These families need special attention, love, and encouragement. Mothers at home need acknowledgment that they are accomplishing some of the greatest work that they'll ever do. They know that, but it is nice to know that others know it as well. Strengthen families.

## Enjoy a Unified Sisterhood

The fifth point of the Relief Society mission statement is to Enjoy a Unified Sisterhood. What a satisfying, hopeful idea that is — to enjoy each other's friendship, benefit from each other's insights! The Lord taught, "If ye are not one ye are not mine." (D&C 38:27.)

A friend told me a story about a visual demonstration of the power of unification. For a Relief Society lesson, a teacher brought in a big fish net and spread it on the floor. When all the sisters came in, she asked them to stand around the fish net and lift together. Then she had some of the sisters raise their hands high. She said, "What happens to this fish net when some of you lift it up? What happens when some of you let go?" They did several things with the fish net. Then she said, "Everyone hold on with both hands and pull it toward you gently. What happens to our net?" It was tight and strong. She said, "Isn't this just like our sisterhood in Relief Society? When we are all pulling together, it comes together in a wonderful way."

I can't think of anything that I could wish more for a sister in Relief Society than that she would feel that kind of bonding, friendship, love, encouragement, and support. Relief Society exists to help us show these feelings for each other.

The aims of Relief Society are nicely summarized in Doctrine and Covenants 123:17: "Therefore, dearly beloved [sisters], let us cheerfully do all things that lie in our power; and then may we stand still [and recognize, appreciate], with the utmost assurance [that we have done all that we can do, that we have blessed the lives of our sisters], to see the salvation of God, and for his arm to be revealed."

# Temple Blessings

"A Million Dollar Temple to Be Built in Cardston, Canada!" came the joyous news in 1913 from the First Presidency of the Church. The temple was to be built of granite, and the groundbreaking would occur at once. By July 1914, my grandfather John F. Anderson, a skilled stonemason from Aberdeen, Scotland, was in Cardston ready to dress stone for the building of this temple. He continued to work on the temple until its completion. His was the honor of acting as the master mason at the laying of the cornerstone in 1915 under the supervision of Apostle David O. McKay. Grandpa laid the last stone to complete the Alberta Temple. He recorded, "It was not the capstone, but a small stone at the front gate entrance."

Grandpa Anderson and my grandmother were two of the first ordinance workers set apart to officiate in the newly completed temple. "This is the greatest calling that has ever come to us," Grandpa wrote in his diary. My grandmother was also set apart as assistant matron of the temple. She recorded, "We were happy of the honor bestowed upon us." Grandpa was caretaker of the temple and served as a patriarch and ordinance worker until his death at age eighty-seven.

My mother and dad were in the first group to be sealed in the Alberta

Temple after its dedication in August 1923. I roller-skated around the temple block, played on the lush lawns when I was a child, strolled the grounds with friends and boyfriends. I did baptisms for the dead there often, getting out of school for part of a morning. We removed our shoes at the door and walked on warm carpet to the cold marble floors of the baptismal room. I was always awed by the massive oxen supporting the font of warm water. When I was in high school I helped Grandpa Anderson by transcribing the patriarchal blessings he gave, doing that in a quiet room in the temple. I received my endowments in the Alberta Temple and was married there, too, surrounded by loving family members, emotionally stirred at the sanctity and beauty of the ceremony.

How grateful I am for temples!

The significance of temples is linked to the foundations of the Relief Society. When the Saints founded Nauvoo, the Lord commanded them to "build a house unto me." (D&C 124:31.) The Saints were so anxious to have this house of the Lord that almost all the men of Nauvoo worked feverishly to complete the building. The women were equally desirous to help in erecting the temple.

In Sarah Kimball's parlor, her seamstress, a Miss Cook, expressed her desire to help. The two joined forces so Miss Cook could sew shirts for which Mrs. Kimball provided fabric. They invited the neighbors to join in this service of making shirts for the temple workmen. This combined effort of the women prompted the organization of Relief Society two weeks later, on March 17, 1842. In future decades several Relief Society general presidents served as matrons of the Salt Lake Temple.

Our temples have always been hallowed. My grandparents, the men and women of Nauvoo, and the Saints who settled the Salt Lake Valley represent the many others who serve so lovingly in the Lord's house. We are told in the vision given to President Joseph F. Smith, documented in Section 138 of the Doctrine and Covenants, that "choice spirits . . . were reserved to come forth in the fulness of times to take part in laying the foundations of the great latter-day work, including the building of the temples and the performance of ordinances therein for the redemption of the dead." (D&C 138:53–54.) Women and men both were reserved for this day to help accomplish this important work of salvation. In the dedication or rededication of a temple, we see the continued fruits of righteousness. Those who attend are the Lord's elect in that part of his kingdom.

Dedication does not only mean dedicating a structure to the work of the Lord. It means dedicating ourselves to the service performed within its walls. Individual blessings will come to those who render such service.

On the Sabbath following the dedication of the Kirtland Temple, the Prophet Joseph told of the Lord's acceptance of the building and quoted His words: "Yea the hearts of thousands and tens of thousands shall greatly rejoice in consequence of the blessings which shall be poured out, and the endowment with which my servants have been endowed in this house." (D&C 110:9.)

It is because of the nature of "the blessings which shall be poured out" that the temple is the most sacred place on the earth. This is one place where we surrender worldly cares and inclinations as we dress in white to prepare, symbolically, to enter the presence of the Lord. In the house of the Lord, we experience a sanctifying process of casting off the world and purifying our hearts before the Lord, and consecrating our lives to him. This is a preparatory process. We are told, "Ye are to be taught from on high. Sanctify yourselves and ye shall be endowed with power." (D&C 43:16.)

What a blessing it is that each time we enter the temple, we have the opportunity to rededicate ourselves to righteous living. The Psalmist asks us, "Who shall ascend into the hill of the Lord? or who shall stand in his holy place? He that hath clean hands, and a pure heart." (Psalm 24:3–4.)

Have you ever gone to the temple when you were fraught with pressure and anxiety and found a respite of peace, a new perspective, answers or impressions to guide you through your problem? I have, and gratefully acknowledge it. I have often thought of the words, "Come unto me, all ye that labour and are heavy laden, and I will give you rest." (Matthew 11:28.)

Nonmembers who visit our temples before they are dedicated are also touched by the spirit of these holy houses. Some of them have commented:

"After seeing this beautiful place, everyone should believe there is a God."

"If someone came up and asked me what I saw and felt, I couldn't describe it in words."

"I really enjoy the serenity of your temple. It is very relaxing and I feel close to God."

A member of the press said in Alberta, "There are two things I'd like to do. Could I go back into the room you call the Garden Room and just sit there? And I'd like to sit in the World Room too."

The covenants we make in the house of the Lord are a great source of learning. I know that making covenants is essential to receiving an endowment of spiritual power and knowledge from God. The temple is a house of learning where the Spirit teaches, when we seek that Spirit.

The endowment itself is an endless opportunity for schooling. All creatures will have an eternal or endless existence, but we are granted the challenge and blessing to know God and Jesus our Savior just as we know each other. Sacred and important information as to the nature and functioning of godhood is revealed to us in the endowment ceremony, and we are imbued with spiritual power.

As I return to the temple to perform the endowment on behalf of others, I am reminded of the steadfastness and enduring nature of covenants. They are a constant in a changing world.

In the temple, we sisters receive all the blessings of the priesthood, not by ordination, but by being as fully endowed with the power of the priesthood as are the men. Both men and women wear the garments of the holy priesthood and make the same sacred covenants with God. They both perform priesthood ordinances, having authority to do so.

James E. Talmage wrote: "It is a precept of the Church that women of the Church share the authority of the Priesthood with their husbands, actual or prospective; and therefore women, whether taking the endowment for themselves or for the dead, are not ordained to specific rank in the Priesthood. Nevertheless there is no grade, rank, or phase of the temple endowment to which women are not eligible on an equality with men." (*The House of the Lord* [Salt Lake City: Deseret Book, 1974], p. 79.)

All faithful women may partake of temple blessings through baptisms for the dead, initiatory work, endowments, or other temple activity. Whether single or married—even if a husband is not worthy, is absent, or is not a member of the Church—each daughter of God may receive her temple blessings in the house of the Lord.

The Lord has promised that he will allow us to live with him again. How often do you contemplate that promise, especially in the temple? It is marvelous to me that if we make and keep our covenants we will be given that privilege. The scriptures give us a foreshadowing, a few whisperings, of the significance of that gift. "When he shall appear we shall be like him, for we shall see him as he is; that we may have this hope; that we may be purified even as he is pure." (Moroni 7:48.) I want to be like my Savior, to see him as he is. I want to qualify for those blessings.

Throughout our great journey of life, we are surrounded with the cloak of his love. I often feel the warmth of that cloak as I serve in the house of the Lord. This love is epitomized for me in the scriptures: "Fear not, little children, for you are mine, and I have overcome the world, and you are of them that my Father hath given me; And none of them that my Father hath given me shall be lost. . . . Wherefore, I am in your midst. . . . Watch, therefore, that ye may be ready." (D&C 50:41–46.)

I testify of the mission of our Savior, of the temple and all it symbolizes, and of the sacred blessings it brings to our lives. The temple has been and ever will be an infinitely significant part of my life. May it ever be a significant part of yours.

# Principles of Visiting Teaching

I n early 1991 I visited Relief Society women in Australia. Wati Martin, one of the Area General Board representatives, told me a wonderful story. She said that when she was younger and a newly married woman, she didn't want to go to Relief Society, but her mother explained to her how the organization worked and why it mattered. They were made visiting teaching companions, and her mother taught her how to give the message and showed her how to be sensitive to individual women in their homes. Then one day her mother said, "Wati, I'm not going to be here with you forever; and when I die, Relief Society will be your mother." Wati told me, "My mother died eighteen years ago, and she was right. Relief Society has become my mother."

Then when I returned home I found this in a letter:

> I would like to share with you two sources of concern and frustration. I feel that for many women, visiting teaching is becoming a square peg in a round hole—a burden rather than a blessing. Our Relief Society president recently told me that only 50 percent of the women in our ward can or will visit teach. I feel it is a program which served its purpose in its time, but in a day of reducing and simplifying in order to

concentrate on essentials, it might be seen as inefficient and even a duplication of efforts.

I want to focus here on the principles of visiting teaching. I want to explain how the pegs fit exactly into the hole. I want to explore how it is that through visiting teaching we act as mothers, sisters, helpers, companions, and friends. Visiting teaching is one of the oldest and most important parts of Relief Society. Shortly after Relief Society was founded in 1842, "a necessity committee" of sixteen members was formed to do friendly visiting. This promise was made to them: "The Spirit of the Lord will help you in it." In Nauvoo, sisters usually walked from one home to another to gather their reports on the condition of the Saints.

A woman who had been a visiting teacher for forty-eight years in southern Utah told this story about her experiences:

> We were having our families then, so often had to take our babies with us. As it would take us most of a day, we were often treated to homemade root beer in the summer, and in the winter the sisters would ask us into the fire to warm up. . . . There were no pavements in those days, and we would have to push the baby buggy through the mud. We would often lose our rubbers and really have a hard time to cross the streets. In the summer it was hot and dusty, but hot or cold, dust or mud, and no matter how busy we were, we always planned to do our teaching on time, and the Lord blessed us in our work. (*The Relief Society Magazine: A Legacy Remembered 1914-1970* [Salt Lake City: Deseret Book, 1982], p. 56.)

Until 1943, visiting teachers accepted contributions for charitable purposes, and one early-day visiting teacher reported:

My partner and I would receive contributions of food, soap, clothing, carpet rags, meat, butter, dried fruits, wild berries, etc. We always carried a basket and a sack. The eggs and perishable produce would be put in the basket and the rest in the sack. Sometimes we would receive so many things that we would have to leave them at the homes and go back the next day. If we came into a home where help was needed, we would often stop on our way to help care for the sick, or give a tired mother a helping hand or take home the unfinished knitting of much-needed stockings. Sometimes, we would return in the evening and sit up with the sick, and at Christmas time, we would see that each family had something special for their holiday cheer. (Ibid.)

Lucy Mack Smith, the mother of the Prophet Joseph, said at the second meeting of Relief Society, "We must cherish one another, comfort one another and watch over one another." I would add, We must nurture, protect, defend, support, cheer, and love one another. As long as we feel this concern and love, visiting teaching will be a successful and important part of who we are as Latter-day Saints.

We should never underestimate the value of a one-on-one visit. Just as women walked around Nauvoo gathering information about the conditions of individuals and families in that early era of the Church, so do sisters in Perth, Australia, and Papeete, Tahiti, walk to homes of their neighbors to visit and care for one another. I think it's exciting to be a part of a worldwide association of sisters who exercise this watchful care over each other. Sometimes when I've gone out visiting teaching I've thought about that, and wondered if maybe women in Manitoba, Canada, or in Mexico or in France or even in the Soviet Union were out doing their visiting teaching at the same time I was. It's quite a concept, to be part of something that is so much bigger than ourselves.

But even more exciting to me is the fact that I can make a difference — I can visit Jesse and Maureen and Lucille and they'll be happy to see me. That's the value of the one-on-one visit. Nothing substitutes for that opportunity of creating an honest, personal relationship that is part of the unified sisterhood we emphasize in our Relief Society mission statement.

I have good visiting teachers. I am not easy to get hold of, but they are pretty steady. They will come at 8:00 A.M. or 9:45 P.M. or on Sunday or catch me by phone, but they're consistent, and one or the other keeps in touch to know if things are all right with me. You might think, "Don't you get enough of Relief Society every day?" It's true that I spend many, many hours a day with the important business of Relief Society; but when my visiting teachers come, they're not talking to me as Sister Jack, Relief Society president, they're talking to me as Elaine — their friend, their neighbor — and that is important. I never get enough of a one-on-one association with my visiting teachers whom I love. I need my visiting teachers, and so do you.

I have heard many questions and interesting interpretations regarding the "new visiting teaching policy." In the 1988 *Relief Society Handbook*, guidelines were given that would allow more flexibility in the visiting teaching program. As you read them, you might ask yourself, What is the intent of the guidelines?

> The work of Relief Society in assisting the bishop to seek
> out and care for the poor and the needy is largely carried out
> through visiting teaching. This selfless service within a loving
> sisterhood can bring both temporal and spiritual blessings. . . .

The Relief Society president assigns a pair of visiting teachers to each sister to act as a support in time of need. Each sister should receive a contact monthly, such as a personal visit, telephone call, or letter. At least once each quarter, these contacts should be in the form of a personal visit. Those with special needs require more frequent contacts than others. These would include those who are new to the Church or the area; those who are less active, single parents, divorced, widowed, or aged; and those with illness, death, or other difficulties in their families. The more active and fully participating sisters may not require the same attention as those with special needs.

In visiting teaching, both the giver and the receiver are blessed and strengthened in their Church activity by their caring concern for one another.

What is the purpose of visiting teaching? Let me pull out some phrases from our own handbook: *selfless service, loving sisterhood*, to *bring temporal and spiritual blessings*. This has not changed and it never will, because it is based on truth.

What *has* changed in visiting teaching is the flexibility given to use a telephone call or a letter, along with a personal visit, as ways to contact sisters. I fear that many of us have looked at the letter rather than the spirit of the law in how we accomplish our visiting teaching. The handbook never said to visit a sister only quarterly or to visit fully active sisters in lesser degrees than we visit the less-active sisters. What it says is that we should reach out in selfless service within a loving sisterhood, and that there is more than one way to do that. Some of our best gospel experiences come to us as we teach one another or as we receive visits.

Let me share with you the story of Sister Ellis. Sister Ellis is ninety-one years old and lives in Adelaide, Australia. When we went to visit her in her home, I was impressed that the woman who greeted us first was her visiting teacher, a young woman in her early twenties who was planning to be married in the fall. Also there was the ward Relief Society president, as well as the stake Relief Society president, who had brought us. All these sisters knew each other and warmly greeted each other as we entered the home. I was impressed to think that there in Adelaide the stake and ward leaders and the visiting teacher all knew Sister Ellis and cared about her welfare. They have the spirit of visiting teaching.

I am sure there is not a woman among us who couldn't write down a wonderful reason for visiting teaching. If we understand the principle so well, why is visiting teaching such a challenge? I think the reason it is a challenge for most of us is because what we *think* and what we *feel* about it are not always the same. Let me share some comments I have heard about visiting teaching from sisters around the world. See if these ring a bell with you:

"We could get 100 percent if we didn't have to keep track of all those women on our rolls that we can never find."

"It seems so stupid to visit my close friends; I feel silly giving them a spiritual message."

"We concentrate on the less active, but sometimes I feel that the sisters who come all the time get ignored—they get all the work and none of the benefit."

"I wish my visiting teachers wouldn't stay so long."

"I wish my visiting teachers wouldn't leave so soon."

"If I could just keep in touch with everyone every three months, I could spend more time."

"My companion's the problem, so I go alone—it's easier."

These common barriers to effective visiting teaching can be overcome, if we approach our callings in the right way. Sometimes all we need is a little rethinking, a little refocusing of our efforts.

If you were to be asked, Who has been an influential person in your life? you might mention all different sorts of people—some family, some teachers, some others—but what they would all have in common is that *they took a personal interest in you*. Why is it that we sometimes have a hard time remembering the value of personal interest when we do our visiting teaching? Visiting teaching is not a perfunctory task—it is not a matter of rushing to a home, leaving a message, and scooting off to our next appointment. It is a matter of building a personal relationship. This is a much harder thing to do. It is also a much more rewarding thing to do.

I remember several years ago when two of my neighbors went to make a second call on a sister in their district that they had missed. After that visit they said, "As long as we're out, let's stop by Helen Peterson's and see how her father is." When Helen opened the door and saw them, she said, "Oh, how did you know? My dad passed away this afternoon." My friend Doral, one of the visiting teachers, told me, "Elaine, we're going to sit at Helen's house during the funeral. For the first time in my life, I felt like a real visiting teacher." Real visiting teaching matters in the lives of individuals.

I don't believe for one minute that a woman who is active in the Church needs visiting teachers any less than a woman who is less active in the Church or even inactive in the Church. We need to be concerned about the individual. One day my counselors and I went downstairs to the Church Office Building cafeteria for lunch. When we showed our ID cards to the woman at the desk, she said, "Oh, did you come to visit teach me?" We said, "No, we really came for a turkey sandwich," and started walking toward the cafeteria line. But she said to me, "I wish you would visit me. I don't have any visiting teachers or home teachers." Now, that stopped me in my tracks, and I went back. "Have you talked to your president?" I said. "Yes," she responded, "and she's the one who says that since I am the stake Relief Society secretary, I don't need any visiting teachers. I have cried to the bishop, too, and he says, 'Oh, we know that you work for the Church and you go to church, that you're faithful; we don't think you need any home teachers,' but, Sister Jack, I do. I need them both."

Now, just as there are situations like this where a woman needs regular visits, so there are circumstances where other types of contact meet the need. In California a young woman commented, "We need to know the program— are you a bad girl if you only use a phone call?" The point is the *need*, which must be met—not how often a woman is visited or what manner is used to visit her. Nothing substitutes for a personal contact, and that is the major criteria by which we should measure our performance as visiting teachers—to be sure that women receive a personal contact that is according to their needs.

Many women need visiting teachers to give them support, reassurance, and comfort. Some, particularly younger women, need role models. Some women are lonely; they just need someone to say hello. Others have no access to priesthood blessings in their home. We can help them to know that a home teacher or a quorum leader is available and concerned about them.

What is the rule about how long people should stay or how long visits should be? I have had wonderful visiting teachers stay five satisfying minutes or two satisfying hours, based on the circumstance. Once my visiting teacher replaced a thermal coupler on my furnace when she found me huddled with my children in front of a fireplace waiting for the repairman.

Sometimes the relationships we build with visiting teachers and with our visiting teaching companions last over the decades. I'll never forget the day that my husband and I arrived with our family at Mount Edgecumbe, Alaska. We had small children. We were stationed in bare government housing with our furniture still five weeks away by boat. At 9:00 A.M. the first day, there was a knock on my door. Standing in front of me with a hot huckleberry pie was a beautiful woman who said, "Hi, I'm Helen Dolenc. Welcome to Mount Edgecumbe. It's so good to have another Mormon family on the island." In those days Mount Edgecumbe wasn't a branch—it wasn't even a twig. I was so grateful for this self-appointed visiting teacher and spent many subsequent days picking berries with her. Helen hasn't changed. One day on my desk appeared some home-canned salmon with this note, signed Don: "Here's some of mother's best from the best mother." Don Dolenc was Helen's only child, and I had given him his first bath. Do I think visiting teaching is rewarding? Absolutely!

How can we best visit teach? Here are a few basic guidelines:

1. Be prayerful.

2. Seek the Spirit. This means praying throughout the month for the women we visit teach—not just five minutes before we go to their house.

3. Show concern by responding in trusting ways, by listening, by risking in sharing our own stories.

4. Give help when needed. Visiting teachers should take the initiative and suggest possible solutions to presidents when they report on the visits they make. My daughter-in-law Gayle's visiting teachers realized when her husband went to Saudi Arabia with the U.S. military forces that they had canceled the newspaper and their membership in a sports club. The visiting teachers shared aerobic tapes and scripture cassettes, and every day a day-old newspaper appeared at Gayle's doorstep.

5. Adapt the message to the sister being visited. The visiting teaching messages in each month's *Ensign* give good gospel information, but they must be adapted so they become part of a sister's life. She should be personally involved in the discussion. I am saddened by stories of visiting teachers who go in and dump a load of their own troubles and concerns on the women they visit. This is not the spirit of the work.

6. Encourage, acknowledge and accept those we visit, with all their concerns. We do not visit homes to judge. We visit homes to help.

7. Schedule visits whenever possible. Granted, we can't always schedule the time we come, but we should be considerate of other people's needs as much as possible and be joyful in the work. Visiting teaching is the gospel in action. It should bring us joy because we are living the law of Christ when we visit teach one another.

8. In visiting teaching we reach out to each other. Hands often speak as voices can't. A warm embrace conveys volumes. A laugh together unites us. A moment of sharing refreshes our souls. We cannot always lift the burden of one who is troubled, but we can lift her so she can bear it well.

Sister Camilla Kimball was an exemplary visiting teacher for more than fifty years. She understood the spirit of this great work when she said: "We are responsible for one another. I help you and you help me. Visiting teaching offers some of the strongest evidence that we are truly willing to serve one another.... All people need to appreciate what life has already given us and realize that we can still give what Christ has directed us to give—service and love." (*The Writings of Camilla Eyring Kimball,* ed. Edward L. Kimball [Salt Lake City: Deseret Book, 1988], pp. 10, 145.)

# *Providing in the Lord's Way*

I have learned many things over the years about the essence of the gospel. Recently I looked up the dictionary definitions of the words *provide* and *charity,* two words that capture that essence. I studied these because *provide* is a word we use often in welfare, and *charity* is a word we use often in Relief Society. It's interesting to consider how similar they are.

As used in the scriptures, *provide* seems to have two basic meanings. One is to prepare and get ready. This seems to be the use in Hebrews 11:40, "God having provided some better thing for us." To provide also means to furnish or supply. Doctrine and Covenants 75:28 talks about "every man who is obliged to provide for his own family." Of course, those meanings are close to each other and sometimes interchangeable.

A look at how the Lord and his prophets use the word *provide* is much more than an exercise in verbiage. It is really an opportunity to understand what the Lord wants us to know and then to do in order to provide in his way. The essence of providing in the Lord's way is twofold; it demands both preparing and furnishing. Sometimes these come together; sometimes they are separate functions. They are both essential to the principles of welfare.

I mention these definitions because they help me define and understand Relief Society and welfare. If we are indeed serious about helping the Saints make ready and have the capacity to furnish their families with the things they need, we must be serious about the principles of charity. And after all, Charity Never Faileth is more than a motto for us in Relief Society, it's our way of life.

Here are some scriptural phrases that discuss elements of charity: "Thou shalt love thy neighbor as thyself." (Matthew 19:19.) "Relieve the oppressed." (Isaiah 1:17.) "Give to the poor." (Mark 10:21.) "Succor those that stand in need." (Mosiah 4:16.) Each of these is stated as a commandment: love, relieve, give, succor. Each is a strong action word—just as vivid and compelling as the word *provide*.

For me, a large part of getting the big picture is getting an understanding of these words. Together they encapsule the essence of Relief Society and welfare.

## Love

I have had many wonderful experiences with men and women throughout the Church. I have traveled through the United States, to Canada, Tahiti, Australia, South Africa, Ghana, and Cote d'Ivoire. I have also met in my office women from Poland, Russia, Czechoslovakia, Germany, Zimbabwe, Korea, Japan, Samoa, Finland, Sweden, Mexico, and more. My testimony has grown as I have observed and heard many happy, sad, and moving stories about how the Saints of God reach out to others.

Raija "Pini" Kemppainen and her husband Jussi are natives of Helsinki, Finland. They serve together in the mission presidency of the Helsinki East Mission. They often go into the republics of the Soviet Union to meet with the fledgling branches of the Church in Vyborg, St. Petersburg, and Moscow. Pini explained to the Relief Society general presidency how difficult it is for new members of the Church in the Eastern bloc countries to learn to administer the programs of the Church. Imagine never having been to church before. Imagine having to shop for the necessities of life two to three hours each day. Imagine three families living in an apartment of 600 square feet. Pini told us that the sisters in Vyborg, a small Soviet community just east of the Finnish border, struggle to care for their families, maintain their homes, work full-time, and establish the Church in their town. These modern pioneers hunger to know what it means to be a Latter-day Saint.

Pini wanted the sisters to know how to visit teach each other. She introduced the concept of visiting teaching with a story about her ten-year-old daughter. It seems the girl came home very upset one day because she could not walk the neighbor's dog. "Well, that's no reason to be upset," Pini commented. "You don't understand," the girl responded. "Two neighbor girls take the dog for a walk to earn money. I do it for the heart." And that's what visiting teaching is—what we do for the heart.

I love that story because it speaks to my heart about the reason why visiting teaching or home teaching matters. I often think what a difference it would make in the neighborhoods of this world if every visiting teacher said before she knocked on a door, "I am making this visit for the heart—my sister's and mine."

The point is that love is the most inviting, memorable, motivating experience in life. I have often thought that perhaps the major reason the Lord told us to love one another is that only through the experience of loving someone can we begin to understand the Lord's love for us. Nothing enriches the soul as much as loving someone else enough to put them first. Nothing makes us better people than the opportunity to care for someone even when it is inconvenient for us. Love—charity—is an eternal law of such magnitude that the prophets have told us if we don't possess it, little else matters. Amulek testified, "If ye do not remember to be charitable, ye are as dross, which the refiners do cast out, (it being of no worth)." (Alma 34:29.)

When I was in Tahiti, a stake Relief Society presidency took me to the home of a woman who has been paralyzed for many years. She gets around her small home by pulling herself on her elbows. She had no visible means of leaving the home, but family members were very much in evidence bringing in the things she needed to live. I was touched by the obvious love between this woman and that presidency. They embraced and kissed each other in greeting. They clasped hands and chatted excitedly in Tahitian. It was a wonderful moment to watch and to feel.

In South Africa a sister conducts a community homemaking class. She invites local women, most of whom are not of our faith, to attend classes in how to use native foods to prepare nutritious meals and how to make items at home that they can sell. Seventy women came the first time she offered this class, ninety the second.

My journal is full of stories like this of loving women and men. Nothing is more central to a true Christian life than demonstrating love for others. Nothing can compensate for lack of love. Nothing is as satisfying as loving others. Nothing is more necessary for our growth than to love and be loved. Nothing, absolutely nothing, is as good as love. If our work is not based on love, it won't matter what it is based on.

## Relieve

I have always been glad that our organization is called the "Relief Society," not the "Benevolent Society." There was some considerable discussion at the founding of Relief Society about the name of the organization. Fortunately, from my point of view, *relief* won out. I guess I like the word so much because it seems so full of action. Relief gets right to the heart of things. The word literally means "removal, lessening, aid, help, and support." When we relieve someone, when we extend relief, we're doing a lot.

Brother and Sister Kissi in Ghana run the Deseret Clinic. They specialize in helping expectant mothers. Sister Kissi, a stake Relief Society president, is a midwife. She teaches about prenatal care and caring for each other. Brother Kissi, a regional representative, is a physician. In their little clinic they teach about relief as much as they provide it. An example of their care is that they cook for patients who must stay overnight. This is unusual in a country where the family is expected to bring in food for patients. The Kissis know that relief comes to mothers and babies in more than one way. They try to relieve both body and spirit, thereby extending the type of relief the Lord intends.

To me relief is a feeling of having all the pressure lifted off. In my visits with women around the world I think the most common refrain is that they feel great pressures. Their welfare needs relate to these pressures, which come primarily from family and economic sources. I find that most women do an admirable job of confronting and conquering their own life pressures. What they need is support. We all know the Church cannot administer so all the Saints are completely relieved of their burdens. But I am convinced that we can minister so the Saints feel relief. We can work to respond more lovingly. We can listen more and say less. We can extend a hand of fellowship, even a hand up when needed. We can let people know in many ways that they are loved, that they matter. I do not suppose it is easy to minister. I do know that to do so is the essence of the gospel.

I have never seen better examples of this Christlike ministering than among the missionary couples who often serve in circumstances far removed from the comforts of life. In Australia I met a couple in Alice Springs. The Alice, as they call it, is in the heart of the outback—smack in the center of Australia. They call it the back of beyond, with good reason. Here six elders serve along with one senior couple. I watched Sister Hansen teach new converts to the Church how to conduct a Relief Society meeting. I watched Elder Hansen help a new branch president organize his presidency. I watched both of them put an arm around every Saint who walked across the threshold of that small branch. Talk about relief. I don't know who felt more of it—the mission president knowing those elders were in good hands, or the branch president knowing he had a good senior companion to help him, or the brand-new convert sister who was a new mother far away from her own mother. The Hansens relieved all of them.

## Give

*Give*—now there's a word for you. Think of all the Lord has given us. I cannot possibly make a complete list, but here are a few of the Lord's gifts to us. He gave his only begotten Son. (John 3:16.) The Savior gave his life for the sheep. (John 10:11.) Through his atonement, the Savior gives us everlasting consolation. (2 Thessalonians 2:16.) The Lord gave the children of Israel a land. (Genesis 12:7.) He gives to us according to our deeds. (Psalm 28:4.) He gives rest. (Matthew 11:28.) He gives and requires much. (Luke 12:48.) Try sometime

*155*

to look up all the scriptures in the Topical Guide about giving. It's a wonderful experience to read about giving as the Lord has done it and as he asks us to do it.

The Lord has told us a lot about giving. But he has also told us through our leaders that we are not required to give what we don't have. I find this doctrine very comforting. I should give according to my circumstances, not yours.

In the context of welfare giving means many other things. It means that we must teach each other the correct principles of giving. I was dismayed recently when I learned that at a Church college, some young Relief Society sisters went to their bishop requesting money because they'd overspent their food budget for the month. It is my hope that a good bishop counseled with those sisters, taking advantage of that opportunity to teach them the correct doctrine about giving and provident living.

We are most blessed because we know that, in fact, giving is a part of our stewardship. The Lord taught, "I, the Lord, . . . built the earth . . . and all things therein are mine." (D&C 104:14.) "Yea, I prepared all things, and have given unto the children of men to be agents unto themselves." (D&C 104:17.) "That every man may give an account unto me of the stewardship which is appointed unto him." (D&C 104:12.)

We need to understand those critical concepts. First, all things are the Lord's and we are stewards over them. When I finally understood this doctrine of stewardship, it was a great moment in my spiritual development. It was something I learned, however. It did not distill as the dews from heaven. When we understand that what we give is in part a measure of our stewardship to the Lord, we can put our giving in a better spiritual context. There is a real freedom in saying from the heart, "All these goods are not mine. They are the Lord's and he has lent me his property." I find that children, youth, and adults are less selfish when they think this way about the goods of this world.

A woman I know has the habit of saying to her children, "I pay for this car, but I don't feel like its owner. I am the steward of it. The Lord has blessed our family with enough money to buy it, but it's our joint stewardship. That means that every time you take a corner fast and leave some of the tire rubber on the street, our stewardship is a little less valuable. Each time you borrow it, it's part of your responsibility to fill it with gas. Just remember, dear, it's our joint stewardship to take care of this car." This is a smart mother. After all, if it's only Mom's car, the teenagers don't feel much responsibility for it. But when everyone has a piece of the responsibility, the thought patterns are different.

It is a true part of human nature that we are more likely to cooperate and participate when we understand how we fit into the big picture. When we understand our responsibilities, it is as if the map descends and at last we can see where we are and where we need to go to reach our destination. In Relief Society we learn about the joys of charitable giving. Such giving emulates the Savior's example and represents obedience to the comandments the Lord has given us.

Some months ago I made a study of several scriptural recountings of times when the people lived in righteousness. In each case the people gave more freely to the poor as they achieved higher levels of righteousness in their personal lives. As the Lord told us in the Doctrine and Covenants, it is possible to provide for the Saints: "And it is my purpose to provide for my saints, for all things are mine. But it must needs be done in mine own way; and behold this is the way that I, the Lord, have decreed to provide for my saints, that the poor shall be exalted, in that the rich are made low." (D&C 104:15–16.) This can only happen when we as individual Saints are willing to give.

## *Succor*

Perhaps the best synonym for the word *succor* is simply *help*. To me, to offer *help* or *succor* means to assist in ways that correct circumstances. While I was in Africa, I learned some new lessons about providing succor from the Waites. Brother Waite is a wiry, retired school headmaster. His wife is a gray-haired dynamo. They took my husband and me to meet some wonderful people in the Ivory Coast. They introduced us to a member family who are refugees from Liberia. The husband, an attorney, was now reduced to tending a few tomato plants, which were the major source of sustenance for his family. He had literally wheeled his mother out of Liberia in a wheelbarrow. The day we met him, his mother had just died. What the Waites gave that sorrowing family was encouragement and support — succor. I've never been anywhere it was more needed or more appreciated.

I have always been grateful that the Lord used the story of the Samaritan as the means of teaching us about loving our neighbors. This story is instructive to me about the concept of succoring. Luke records: "A certain Samaritan . . . saw him [and] he had compassion on him, and went to him." This Samaritan was a man whose heart had already been softened so that it quickly filled with compassion when he saw a man in need. The Samaritan was also an observer. He saw and felt.

The story continues: "[the Samaritan] went to him, and bound up his wounds, pouring in oil and wine, and set him on his own beast, and brought him to an inn, and took care of him." The Samaritan was a man of action, knowledge, and skill. He knew how to assess a situation and was resourceful in creating a solution to a problem.

Jesus told us further: "And on the morrow when he departed, he took out two pence, and gave them to the host, and said unto him, Take care of him; and whatsoever thou spendest more, when I come again, I will repay thee." (Luke 10:33–35.) The Samaritan looked for long-term solutions, acted with care and responsibility, and still fulfilled his other obligations.

I'm sure you recognize the principles demonstrated in this story as the principles of welfare. Modern-day Samaritans, all of us must be men and women who see, feel Christlike love, know how to act, and possess skill and knowledge. We must know how to assess a situation and create solutions. We must follow through, attempting to act with the care and responsibility the Lord asks of us.

A friend told me recently of a family her son met in Brazil while he was on his mission. The father had been a bishop there and had done well financially. The parents felt, however, that their children would benefit from the educational system of the United States. Moving to New York, they undertook the cleaning of homes and office buildings to support their large family. Because of limited English skills, they could find no other work. They were involved in their ward and served faithfully in every assignment. A son was months away from a mission call when he became ill. Tests showed that a major operation was needed, but the family had no money and no insurance. The parents did not know what to do, but decided not to counsel with their bishop about this matter. They were embarrassed to be in this situation and felt uncomfortable taking any money from the Church.

One day shortly after the parents had made their decision not to involve the Church authorities in their problem, the visiting teachers came. One of the visiting teachers was also the ward Relief Society president. When the sister discussed her son's health, this sensitive president asked about their ability to pay for medical care. Then it all came out—the fears, the reluctance, the embarrassment. The president explained that the welfare system was put in place to succor those in need. She talked with this mother about the importance of being receivers so others could have the blessing and opportunity of giving. An appointment was made with the bishop and appropriate help given.

We take turns being givers and receivers. For most of us it is infinitely more comfortable to be the giver, but sometimes it's ours to receive so others have the growth that comes only from giving the type of succor demonstrated by the Samaritan.

Welfare is not just a program to be administered by the Relief Society president and the bishop. It is individuals giving what they have to give, meeting the specific needs of their brothers and sisters. May each of us recommit to loving, relieving, giving, succoring, and providing in the Lord's way.

# Personal Vision

# Example in the Home

I had a friend who was teaching a child development class at Brigham Young University about fifteen years ago. One day she said, "Elaine, you and Joe must have something special you do in raising your boys. Will you come to my class and tell us what you've done to achieve the results you have?"

I was flattered that she would ask. When I told my oldest son, Dave, that she had asked me to come, he said, "Doesn't she want us to come too?" I said, "No, I don't think so." He continued, "I don't know why not. After all, we're what make you look good." Which brings up a sound leadership principle: no leader is any better than the ones he serves.

*Love* to me is a synonym for home and family. One day I asked my yound son Eric, "What color is love?" He replied, "Pink, because that's the most prettiest color there is."

Husband and wife must love the Lord and love each other. This love fulfills the two greatest commandments, upon which hang all the law and the prophets. "Thou shalt love the Lord thy God with all thy heart, and with all thy soul, and with all thy mind. This is the first and great commandment. And the second is like unto it, Thou shalt love thy neighbour as thyself." (Matthew 22:37–39.) Nothing is more important in a family than having a good mate, being able to share with that person, having the same goals and a united feeling of what you are trying to accomplish. The art of living together happily is perhaps one of the greatest of all arts. *Having* and *being* the right mate are the foundation for all else in the family.

We hear a lot about how important love is with our children, but I believe love is effective only as it is coupled with action. Says the writer of Proverbs, "Train up a child in the way he should go: and when he is old, he will not depart from it." (Proverbs 22:6.) To *train* implies to do something; that is a commanding statement which puts love into action. Sometimes I find that I am trained more easily than the child—I wonder if I'm the trainer or the trainee. But I know action is necessary if I love my children. I have a firm enough testimony to realize the responsibility I have and the importance of the goal of true happiness.

Happiness results when we can feel ourselves progressing, continually growing, learning, changing, and expanding our outlook—being able to see that we are not the same people we were last year. Education is important in the home because it is one way to accomplish this progression, and also because it is an eternal concept. "It is impossible for a man to be saved in ignorance." (D&C 131:6.)

All four of our boys were in college at one time, two at home and two away from home. I remember well the years Dave was applying for medical school. I knew what the odds were for his acceptance and how much it meant to him. Knowing how disappointed he would be if he did not make it, I used to think, "Don't want to go to medical school, Dave. Don't let yourself in for that disappointment again. Want to be a mortician instead!" And yet I admired his integrity and his aspirations and that he worked toward his goal despite the odds.

I realized that we couldn't protect him from every blow or disappointment. In fact, during this time I saw the role of adversity in strengthening character and increasing compassion. I believe in this concept, but it's hard to let my children experience it. To let them progress on their own, accepting failure when necessary, takes a lot of generosity and love.

Our second son, Bill, didn't want to go to medical school. He said his college class was full of pre-med students working only for A grades, and that he enjoyed the learning process too much to be caught in that hassle. "Enjoy the learning process." What joy that idea has brought to me; what joy it brings to Bill and also to the two brothers following him.

Bill has a son of his own now. In a letter he was telling of the latest accomplishment of that common, ordinary, perfect grandchild and said, "James imitates me so directly that it is almost scary." It doesn't scare me. The same boy that imitates his father's taste in dogs and books is going to imitate Bill's style of humor, his desire for excellence, his method of praying.

Often we expect children to do all the learning in a family, without realizing that constant growth is necessary for each of us. Parents set the example in every area of life, including continued learning. Joe is constantly updating and improving his knowledge in his profession. Through my church callings I have tried to keep abreast of women's topics and Relief Society curriculum. I have become proficient in a sport. We study the scriptures. My boys see this and share in our progress as we rejoice in theirs. A big boost one summer came when Eric was hitting balls to me on the tennis court and said, "Hey, Mom, you're not bad for a beginner. Try it again." Perhaps that was a little thing, but in family living, the little things are often the big things. The progress we make here is not only for now but for the eternities.

I appreciate the example set by the older boys for the younger. When Eric left on his mission, Gord was being especially helpful to his dad in the yard one day. When I commented on this, he replied, "I have to help now that Eric's gone." He had moved from the shade into the sunlight of bright example.

I also appreciate the example set by a grandfather. My dear father above all taught me the dignity of work, the rewards of self-reliance, and the joys of service. Even in the eighty-seventh year of his life he was happiest with some widow's lawn to cut or bushes to trim or snow to shovel. My children saw this — and saw how independent Grandpa was, wanting to still do everything himself even when his ambitions outpaced his physical abilities. Our whole family's attitude about work came from him. We have rarely had to pay college tuition, because our boys worked themselves through or earned scholarships.

Family members can give great encouragement to each other. In the close circle of love, words of correction and suggestions are somehow softened, cushioned with caring. I maintain that a woman has to have a healthy self-esteem to survive living in a family of four boys. Actually, they stimulate me to build self-esteem. I find that it is more important for me to achieve in the eyes of my family than for anyone else. Conversely, it is important for me to let them, more than anyone else, know that I appreciate their accomplishments.

Once I had asked Joe to do a household chore for me so I could concentrate on a troubling assignment I had been given. He responded, "Okay, I'll do that chore, but I don't want to ever hear you say again that you're not smart enough to fulfill that assignment. You are smart enough; you can too do it." Maybe that would not be encouraging to you, but his words helped me feel I really could accomplish that job.

Our family has fun together. Joe has always geared his free time to activities the whole family could enjoy, so we did a lot of things together. I've gone through cycles of learning, as Joe's teaching the boys has also taught me.

Through the years, I have found joy in watching our boys learn to put the needs of others before their own. I remember Bill helping Eric with math in eighth grade. Eric was rebellious because he wanted answers and Bill insisted on methods, and they had some stormy sessions. Bill was willing to help if Eric appreciated it, but he didn't like wasting his time if Eric wasn't going to listen. Then I remember report card time and the look of great satisfaction on Eric's face when he came in the door exclaiming, "I got an A in math!" Then, recognizing the reason behind it, he added, "Thanks to Bill."

I think of the two older boys fussing about the difficulties of driving to the University of Utah together and waiting for each other. I realized that Dave, who worked each night until midnight and then studied afterward, got up in time to take Bill to a 7:45 A.M. class all during the dark, snowy winter quarter although Dave's own first class did not start until 9:20. And I also noticed that Bill was always up and had the snow scraped off the windshield and the motor warm when Dave came out of the house.

President Spencer W. Kimball said, "Heaven is a place, but also a condition; it is home and family. It is understanding and kindness. It is interdependence and selfless activity. It is quiet, sane living; personal sacrifice, genuine hospitality, wholesome concern for others." (*Ensign,* December 1971, p. 39.) In Doctrine and Covenants 130:2 the Lord tells us, "That same sociality which exists among us here will exist among us there [when the Savior comes], only it will be coupled with eternal glory."

Our homes should be places where family members get along well and bring out the best in one another. Our success will largely be determined by how faithfully we focus on living the gospel in the home. A parent's role is to provide leadership and example.

I'd rather be a mother than anything else. When Dave used to call from Washington and became immediately engrossed in discussing a medical concept with Joe, when the whole family jumped with excitement over the important letter that came from the First Presidency with a mission call, when I watched the adoration with which the youngest boy followed the oldest in everything he did, when I saw the tenderness with which the oldest, age ten, held a newborn baby brother in his arms, then indeed my cup ran over, and I wanted our family life to go on forever. The Lord has outlined the plan and told us what to do so that it can. I thank him for the glimpse of heaven I have now in my family, and for the promises that it can continue.

# Rings of Growth

**W**hen Christmastime rolls around each year, I envision the bushy, fragrant pine trees we had in my parents' home in Canada. My dad had a friend who cut trees fresh from the nearby mountains and hauled them to our home on a horse-drawn sleigh. These huge trees brushed the ceiling and filled the corner of our living room with branches heavy enough to hold our wrapped presents. To me the tree represents everything good about the season: my home, the love we share, family togetherness, and Christmas itself.

It was exciting to be a bride living in Staten Island, New York, during the Christmas season of 1949. Both my husband, Joe, and I worked in Manhattan and spent our limited free time happily exploring the city together. We were having a wonderful time. Life was good.

Early in December we received a letter from Fred, an old neighborhood friend of Joe's, telling us that he would be in New York for three days on his way home from a two-year mission. We knew that he had served in Czechoslovakia for eighteen months and had completed his mission in England, but we were oblivious to the conditions in Europe at that time. We were light-hearted, carefree, and eager to share our Christmas cheer with an old friend.

Fred arrived a sobered young missionary. He told us of being forcibly expelled from Czechoslovakia, of scarce food and dwindling medical supplies in the country, of the devotion of the Latter-day Saints and how he hated to leave them. He was unsettled and troubled by the oppressive events he had witnessed in Europe.

It was two weeks before Christmas. While I was preparing a special turkey dinner the evening after Fred arrived, I suggested that he and Joe go on the bus to get a Christmas tree for the bedroom of our small two-room apartment. I was anxious to have a tree. While Joe and Fred were gone, I envisioned a beautiful, full tree, reminiscent of those at home.

When I heard Joe and Fred coming up the stairs, I rushed to see what they had brought. Joe held the New York tree—small enough to be carried in one hand. I was shocked. This Christmas tree would never do! "It will be just fine for the table," Joe said. A tree that would fit on a table? A table tree was simply not acceptable! I pointed out the only solution, "Take it back and get a bigger one." Apparently Joe sensed how important it was to me because with minimal protest he and Fred took the small tree back on the bus to exchange it for a larger one. The six-foot tree with sparse branches and short needles that ended up at the foot of the bed was not very beautiful even with decorations, but at least it was a tree that could bridge the transition from the Christmases of the past to the establishing of our own family memories and traditions.

Seven years later our home was in southeast Alaska. Joe and I and our first two sons, David, six, and Bill, four, lived in government housing at the edge of a large area of muskeg—a spongy, swampy bog covered with moss and small plants. Ponds of water, a few pine trees, small shrubs, and skunk cabbage were scattered across this fertile area.

Because they stood alone, muskeg pine trees were usually well formed and symmetrical — perfect for Christmas trees. One afternoon close to Christmas we decided to create a family tradition by chopping our own fresh Christmas tree. We took an axe and a saw and walked to the edge of the muskeg, squishing through the tundra. We examined each tree along the way. Finally, some distance into the bog, we found the perfect one. Joe hacked off the lower branches so he could reach the thick trunk with his saw. Dave, Bill, and I held branches out of the way while he worked at felling the tree. When it toppled over, we were delighted. Dragging the tree was too much for the boys, so I took them on ahead, carefully picking our footing while Joe pulled the tree by himself through the thick, goopey bog. When next I looked, Joe was in the soggiest part of the muskeg to the top of his boots. He tried to pull one foot onto solid ground but only succeeded in burying the other foot deeper into the guck. No matter which foot he tried to extract, he sank further. He couldn't find a solid base. To our horror, he was slowly sinking into the ground!

"Stay where you are, kids," I said. "I'm going to help Dad." Joe yelled, "Stay back! I'll catch my breath and get out of this." Fortunately the branches of the bushy tree had spread over the marshy area; Joe braced himself on the branches and struggled to firmer ground. He was exhausted. He pulled the tree to the edge of the muskeg with the last of his energy and left it there until he could borrow a truck to transport it the rest of the way to our house.

It had been a harrowing experience, but what a tree we had! It was exactly the kind you would choose to put in City Hall. When we got home, we could hardly pull it through the door. Although that tree hadn't filled much of the muskeg, it bumped against the ceiling and nearly touched all four walls of our living room. We chopped off branches from the back of the tree, shoved it toward the corner, then hacked off more branches until it was finally stuffed into the space where it belonged. The lopsided tree fit perfectly with the help of wires to hold it up. We have never had a more magnificent tree. Nor have I ever had a more fatigued husband! Joe said, "In the future, whatever price you have to pay for a tree, pay it. It is worth it!"

Much as I love fragrant, green trees, I followed the fashion in the early sixties and decided to flock our tree. I thought the natural look of a tree after a snowstorm would be a wonderful addition to our Christmas decor. With a do-it-yourself flocking kit that attached to my vacuum cleaner, I was sure I could create a beautiful tree for much less than a tree cost on a lot. I decided that I would do the job right where the tree would stand so none of the flocking would be disturbed. I connected the vacuum to the powdery flocking material and the bottle of water and turned on the power. It worked! Synthetic snow made the tree look like a winter wonderland. As I finished and stepped back to admire my Currier and Ives tree, I noticed that the wall, the sofa, the piano, and the chairs were also part of my winter wonderland. We had a spectacular tree, but snow removal that year continued into June. The following year I remembered Joe's advice in Alaska and paid the price for a tree someone else had flocked.

Last year I didn't send Joe for a tree; I didn't flock one myself; I didn't even buy a Christmas tree. My children have moved to homes of their own, and I used other decorations to bring the festive feelings of Christmas into our home. It was a different kind of Christmas for me. Even without a tree, the feelings that Christmas trees symbolize seemed more real to me than ever before. I basked in the warmth created by years of family togetherness around our trees. A thousand memories fill my heart at Christmastime — memories that have grown and matured into a deeper understanding that the peace and goodwill brought to earth with the birth of the Savior are the basis for all the good things Christmas means. I reflected upon the New York "return-the-tree" season of 1949 and thought how blessed we were to have had the luxury of worrying about the size of our tree when so many people had no means at all. I remembered my two little boys, now fathers, and laughed about Joe's skirmish with a muskeg bog in Alaska. I thought about the many fashions of the holidays: how flocked trees, like wide collars, come and go, but the spirit of Christmas does not change.

# *Heritage*

ne year, while I was painting the walls in my downstairs hall after having con- vinced my husband to help me in our first venture of wallpapering the ceiling, I was thinking with satis- faction of all the rooms and furniture I had painted for our homes. I wondered if my mother knew what ambition and skills she had passed on to me—if she knew that forty years later I would be doing the same things I had seen her do. Then I realized that I have read the same books aloud to my children that my mother read to me. I cook the same desserts Mother did. I use the same expressions.

Although heritage is a personal thing, perhaps you can relate my thoughts to your experiences, and we can share our common legacy as inheritors of traditions and values from the past. I am fascinated by the practical traditions— methods for home doctoring, for gardening and cooking, for decorating and sewing—that mothers pass on to their children. I am also struck by the value systems and the spiritual heritage that enrich our lives. These come both from the ancestors whose names we know and from the scriptural foremothers and fathers we reverence. It is important for us to assess these traditions, because we are in the process of passing on to the next generation our own ways of thinking, feeling, and doing. Will these children remember us with thanks for our dedication to a good cause, to eternal values?

What traits and talents did I inherit? My mother was not what you'd call an artsy-craftsy person, but she didn't sit idle. She was resourceful, and spent much of her time in what we would call recycling. She called it "making over" or "redoing." Her sewing machine was always out. As I think back on my made-over dresses, I remember especially how I loved a red taffeta formal that was made for me from my sister's. And my sister Jean cherishes the memory of a bathrobe made from Grandma's old grey flannel robe, newly trimmed in bright red velvet. Mother did the painting at our house, renewed the old iron-posted bedstead for our newly remodeled bedroom, and could always make a meal out of bits and pieces in the icebox.

Many family traits and ways of doing things come from our heritage, though we're often not conscious of their origins. In me it's the streak of economy, the thrill of getting a bargain, the unique work ethic we developed growing up in southern Alberta. We had to preserve and prepare for the long, cold winter. My sister Jean said, "I've given away my canning bottles three times! But this is my heritage. I can't let things go to waste. I *have* to can." From my heritage too comes an appreciation for the out-of-doors: the wheat fields of Alberta, Old Chief Mountain, patches of yellow buttercups, and purple shooting stars.

Even though some of our heritage passes to us unconsciously, even more we receive because our parents and grandparents consciously wanted to preserve all that was good in their lives, improve upon it, and pass it on to us. Isn't that exactly what we want to do for our children? We want to give them the most valuable things we have. In some ways we can gather up our heritage and offer it to our children.

When the pioneers came to southern Alberta, life was a constant struggle. It was all they could do to provide the basic needs for their families. Yet these pioneers were not satisfied merely to have functional things; they, especially the women, longed for beautiful things too. With imagination and ingenuity and very little else, they created a corner of culture and beauty. They did this in many ways, primarily through their handiwork.

The early settlers made every stitch of clothing and household linens by hand. Practically every article had embellishments of tatting, embroidery, crocheting, or homemade lace. Because there weren't many patterns, women drew on their imaginations and made up their own. Sometimes they borrowed a finished item from a neighbor, "to take a pattern off it." Even when the same pattern was used by many people, the results were individual and distinctive.

Although patchwork is a very old craft, it has become a bridge across generations—an example of culture being passed on. Women used to trade swatches of material with their neighbors in order to get colors and fabrics they needed to finish their patchwork designs. They could proudly point to the piece that was Ellie's Sunday dress or Aunt Lucy's taffeta skirt that she brought from England. Sometimes a thoughtful mother would save bits from her daughter's dresses as she grew up, then piece them all together into a memory quilt for the girl's trousseau. I have friends today who have done the same thing.

It seems that women of every age and time with talented hands have expressed their inherent desire to create and to add something of their own to everyday items. For example, for generations women have been making a statement about the world in which they live through quilt making. Modern quilts reflect technological advances with synthetic blends and bonded batts. Rather than pieces gleaned from the scrap bag, quilts today are usually made from purchased fabric, often with patterns that eliminate the need for marking. With less intricate designs, we tie or machine stitch for "instant" quilts. In this way, we're saying, "I'm busy car-pooling children, taking university classes, learning tennis. Times are good; materials are plentiful." Someday our granddaughters will read this history from our handiwork as they decode the quilts we pass on to them.

Life on a farm forty years ago was demanding on a woman. Even there, my Aunt Antris created her corner of beauty when she planted rows and rows of bounteous vegetables. Beyond the vegetables, she added asters and bells of Ireland, with sweet peas on the fence. People in Cardston nursed geraniums into bloom in their south windows during the cold winter months, red blossoms bringing some brightness into their lives. In our home, cactus blooming at Christmastime was the wonder of the winter.

These townspeople welcomed culture. Some may remember the chautauqua, which was a circuit of traveling lectures and concerts and recitals, performing between about 1903 and 1930 in a large tent in our town. The chautauquas brought a taste of culture to the frontier. In addition, we children had music lessons. We learned about literature and drama. Though we were not New York City or even Toronto, we looked beyond the necessities of life to those things that lifted us and added refinement.

An important part of my heritage is homemaking. To a Latter-day Saint woman, the word *homemaking* has great significance. Since every task performed in her home, whether she lives alone or with a family, is done in the framework of eternity, this demands the best she has to offer. Homemaking includes the creation of beauty, the encouragement of culture, the nurturing of warm family relationships. It also includes the constant concern of every provident homemaker, ancient or modern, for feeding, clothing, and caring for that family.

The provident homemaker is described for all time in the thirty-first chapter of Proverbs: "Who can find a virtuous woman? for her price is far above rubies. . . . She is like the merchants' ships; she bringeth her food from afar. She riseth also while it is yet night, and giveth meat to her household, and a portion to her maidens." (Proverbs 31:10, 14–15.)

My Grandmother Low was this kind of a provident homemaker. I try to be too. Our concerns have been the same, but our methods of providing "meat for our household" have differed. One of my uncles wrote this about Grandmother Low's homemaking ability:

> As father was a bookkeeper and was Stake and Tithing Clerk he knew very little about livestock and farming, but mother was of good farm stock and did much of the managing as well as the work.
>
> I would certainly pay tribute to mother for her ability to take care of a large family as she did all the housework and feeding of an always hungry bunch of kids. Mother made all the clothes, knitted the socks and mittens, made our underwear from grey flannel, as well as milked cows, churned the butter and sold it, raised chickens, ducks and turkeys, was a counselor in the Relief Society and would gather wheat for them from all the neighboring farms.

Grandmother was also a midwife. As hard as all that work she did sounds, is any less required of me? I don't have to do the same physical things Grandma Low did, but I have to be just as industrious, just as compassionate, just as frugal, just as prepared for the winter as she was. This is my heritage.

"She considereth a field, and buyeth it: with the fruit of her hands she planteth a vineyard. She girdeth her loins with strength, and strengtheneth her arms. She perceiveth that her merchandise is good: her candle goeth not out by night. She layeth her hands to the spindle, and her hands hold the distaff. She stretcheth out her hand to the poor; yea, she reacheth forth her hands to the needy." (Proverbs 31: 16–20.)

These are the teachings of the gospel to me today: "I ask you earnestly, have you provided for your family a year's supply of food, clothing, and, where possible, fuel? The revelation to produce and store food may be as essential to our temporal welfare today as boarding the ark was to the people in the days of Noah." (Ezra Taft Benson, *Conference Report,* October 1987, p. 61.)

In her eighties, the prophet's wife, Sister Camilla Kimball, surprised her friends by leaving a study club a little early one spring afternoon. When asked why, she said, "I've got to go home and plant my carrots." One friend asked, "Camilla, do you mean to tell me you plant a garden?" "Of course," she replied, "the prophet has asked us to. Can I do anything less?"

One summer my eighty-four-year-old dad bottled 110 quarts of fruit. Can I do anything less?

I can vividly remember walking up the wooden path to Grandma Anderson's house, opening the door to the smell of finnan haddie or gooseberry pie. On walking into the living room, I usually saw her sitting in her oak armchair at a dropleaf table covered with genealogy sheets. Spread out before her would be correspondence with stamps on it from Great Britain, boxes of papers, an open ink bottle, and a five-cent pencil sharpener. She spent hours researching, corresponding, and copying by hand the names of her ancestors. At her death, her records were passed to her daughter, my mother, who charged me to continue the work. A few years ago, when I got out her records to sort them, I kept thinking, "Surely there must be more. This couldn't have been all Grandma did!" It was all, but her "all" was done without computers or even typewriters, without air mail or special libraries. Her "all" was total dedication to the scripture: "And he shall plant in the hearts of the children the promises made to the fathers, and the hearts of the children shall turn to their fathers." (Joseph Smith–History 1:39.)

Grandma turned to her ancestors in love and concern, and in so doing she set an example that became a valuable heritage passed on to me. If I took my family to the family history library today, we could probably research Grandma's lifetime of genealogy work in three or four hours. But her work, of course, is done, and we have new challenges in research that will take *our* total dedication.

"Her children arise up, and call her blessed; her husband also, and he praiseth her. Many daughters have done virtuously, but thou excellest them all." (Proverbs 31: 28–29.)

In what other ways does our heritage remind us to be dedicated and self-reliant? Health matters are a concern in every generation. We are expected to handle the sickness of family members with care and competence. Can you imagine the feeling of helplessness and terror a woman on the frontier felt when one of her family was struck with whooping cough, smallpox, or diphtheria? She was often isolated, no professional care was available, and she had to use anything she thought might help to save the lives of her loved ones. Sometimes her remedies worked; sometimes they didn't.

My grandmother's remedies now make me smile. Have you heard of using hot onion juice to cure earache? Remember mustard plasters and ginger tea? I certainly remember asafetida placed in a bag and tied around a person's neck. Even though it was dreadfully smelly, some people wore the bag all year, every year, no matter what the season or their state of health, because it was sure to ward off illness. My dad told me about swabbing blue vitriol on the throat as a preventive measure against diphtheria. "I believe it worked, too," I remember Dad saying. "We never got diphtheria."

In times of illness, the most important things frontier women relied on were faith and prayer and healings through the blessings of the priesthood. Many diaries and journals testify of the effectiveness of prayer in the home. My own grandmother recorded in her journal:

> Johnnie was taken so sick at five years old with a very severe case of scarlet fever that everyone thought he was dying, and if he lived, it would be a miracle. The doctor gave him up. Everyone who saw him and knew his case had no hope of his recovery; however, his father and I had faith, and fasted and prayed for days to the Lord to spare his life. He had many complications and was even paralyzed. He could not speak for three weeks and had to learn to crawl and walk all over again. We were so glad when we heard him try to say his first words, "Aunt Betsy" as he was very fond of her, and she was near to help us nurse him night and day. He did recover and fulfilled his mission to the world.

Modern medicine has eliminated many of the diseases that were so dreaded in the early days, but the exercise of faith in healing has not changed. Diaries and journals still record the effectiveness of prayer.

My heritage has prepared me for the opportunities that have come in my life. I am sure that you feel the same about your heritage. Our Father in heaven is using us to advance his work on the earth, in preparing his children to receive Jesus Christ and to live by the principles of the gospel.

Once a daughter tried to express her gratitude to her aged mother for having cared so much about her that at great sacrifice she had provided the daughter rich opportunities for her development. How could she ever pay back? The mother smiled and said with astonishment in her voice, "Why, don't you know, Anne, how you repay? You care as much *and more* for the next generation."

Something of ourselves lives on from generation to generation. "The seeds . . . implanted by the family of one's birth, are ready to sprout as soon as one sets up a family of one's own." (Michael Novak, *Harper's*, April 1976, p. 40.)

What we are is passed on from one generation to another. We influence all those we have contact with, not just immediate family, and they influence us.

"Let every [woman] esteem [her sister] as [herself] and practice virtue and holiness before me." (D&C 38:24.) When we regard each other as equals and openly accept each other, we will relate heart to heart because the Lord will magnify our love and our vision and we will see as he sees.

# Index